Sɪnn Féin

The First Election 1908

By

Ciarán O Duibhir

Series Editor

Proinnsíos Ó Duigneáin

NORTH LEITRIM · HISTORY SERIES ·

Nọ 4

Published by

Drumlin Publications

Nure, Manorhamilton, Co. Leitrim (072) 55237

Published in Ireland in 1993 by
Drumlin Publicatons

© Ciarán O Duibhir

ISBN   1 873437 02 1

Original letters from O'Mara and Redmond Papers reproduced
by kind permission of the National Library.

Cover by Nicole Thoma-Gallagher

**Published by Drumlin Publications, Nure,
Manorhamilton, Co. Leitrim, Ireland (072) 55237**
Printed by Colour Books, Dublin

Sinn Féin

The First Election 1908

Acknowledgements

Any study of this nature is dependent on support, encouragement and assistance of many kinds. I wish to express my gratitude to all those who assisted me in completing 'Sinn Fein – The First Election', which is largely based on a dissertation I submitted to the History Department of Carysfort College of Education. Inevitably any list will not be complete but among those to whom I now say 'thanks' are: Michael Ryan, formerly of the History Dept., Carysfort College, Mrs P. Wilson R.I.P., John O' Hara, Brian Colreavy, Gerry Lally, my parents Agnes and Tomas O'Duibhir, Michael McTernan, Strafford-Wayne, Pennsylvania; Patrick Meehan, Portlaoise; Alice Dolan Topping, St. Louis; Suzanne Starke Kline, St. Louis and the staffs of the following libraries, Carysfort College, Sligo Regional Technical College, Sligo, Leitrim, Louth (Drogheda Branch), Fermanagh County Libraries and The National Library of Ireland.

Ciarán ODuibhir

Contents

Market Street, Killycloghet.

Introduction

Leitrim North forever, neath the flag of green and gold;
Strike for liberty from the centre to the sea as in days of old.
Come one, come all, come great, come small, our forces help
  to swell
Let your Watchword be, for Meehan and liberty, 'Neath the
  banner of the U.I.L.

The Nationalist Members of Parliament found themselves badly divided after the death of Parnell in October 1891 and with the defeat of Gladstone's Second Home Rule Bill in the House of Lords, 1893, they became largely irrelevant in the House of Commons. The division in the ranks was essentially between those who had supported Parnell and those who had opposed him. John Redmond was leader of the Parnellites who were very much a minority, having won just nine seats in the 1892 General Election. However, even among the anti-Parnellites who numbered seventy one in 1892, there were two factions – one led initially by Justin McCarthy and from 1896 by John Dillon. T. M. Healy was leader of the second group. The main cause of this division was the role the Catholic Church should play in politics. Healy advocated clerical involvement while the Mc Carthy-Dillon faction favoured a party not dictated to by the Church.[1]

Soon after the defeat of his second Home Rule Bill, Gladstone retired as leader of the Liberals and his successor, Lord Rosebery had little regard for Home Rule.[2] In effect this meant that the Liberals, whose support for Home Rule was necessary if it was ever to see the light of day, had, now, temporarily at least, abandoned the idea. This, and the success of the Conservatives in subsequent elections, resulting in their holding power for the next ten years, isolated the nationalist members. The isolation felt by the Irish members was summed up by Redmond in 1894 when he said that they were, "face to face with the ruin of the Home Rule cause........"any measure of autonomy must be hung up until the English cared to give it".[3]

For their part the Conservative governments adopted what could be described as a reasonably benign attitude to Ireland. This has been called a policy of "Conservative Unionism" as well as "Killing Home Rule by Kindness". The thinking behind the policy was that if some materialistic desires were satisfied, Home Rule would cease to be an issue[4]. Killing home rule by kindness resulted in many constructive and valuable reforms, e.g. the establishment of the Congested Districts Board; of the Department of Agriculture and Technical Instruction and in the passing of the *Wyndham Land Act* and the *Local Government Act.* Based on local government in Britain,the Irish *Local Government Act 1898* paved the way for the introduction of County Councils, Urban District Councils and Rural District Councils elected on a wide franchise. This gave the local Catholic middle class a greater say in local administration, heretofore dominated by the landlord ascendancy class.[5]

When eventually the nationalist members of Parliament reunited in 1900 under Redmond, they did so for a variety of reasons. In 1898 William O Brien had founded the United Irish League primarily to campaign for land reform. The League grew quickly. In 1900 it had 63,000 members. A year later this figure had swelled to 100,000.[6] To the ailing parliamentary party it offered a massive organisation which could work the constituencies in the same manner as the Irish National League had done for Parnell. Although O'Brien had hoped that the League would be the stronger partner, it soon became obvious that it was really the members of parliament who devised and dictated policy. While they had to account annually to a National Convention held under the auspices of the U.I.L., this was no more than a rubber stamping authority.

Other factors which may have influenced party unity, were the 1798 centenary celebrations in 1898 and the Boer War in South

Africa. Compared to the spirit of the men of 1798 and the stiff resistance the Boers were then offering to British imperialism, the squabbles of the Irish parliamentarians appeared very petty. However despite Redmond's success in uniting most of the Irish Nationalists there remained some maverick M.Ps. T. M. Healy refused to dissolve the People's Right Association, which he had established during the split. He was formally expelled in December 1900. Another to leave the party was William O Brien, who departed in 1904 for reasons outlined below [7].

However, if at this time the Irish Parliamentary party was irrelevant in the House of Commons, Irish society was experiencing changes. Sir Horace Plunkett was responsible for many of these. Plunkett was a Protestant Unionist landowner who started a co-operative society at Doneraile in County Cork in 1899. In 1894 he founded the Irish Agricultural Organisation Society, which by 1903 had 800 branches with a membership of eighty thousand. The I.A.O.S. looked after the marketing of produce, the manufacture of butter and the supply of fertilisers. Most importantly it provided credit through its land banks.[8] Plunkett was also one of the Unionists involved in the *All-Ireland Committee*, founded in February 1897 with the support of John Redmond and T.M. Healy, to discuss what action could be taken in protest at the findings of a Royal Commission which suggested that Ireland had been seriously over-taxed by the Union. Plunkett was largely responsible for the establishment of the Recess Committee, consisting of Liberal Unionists and some nationalists, which in 1896 issued a report recommending more government involvement in the financial and administrative development of agriculture. This led in 1899, to the setting up of the Department of Agriculture and Technical Instruction. This new Department provided lecturers to give advice on horticulture, poultry-breeding and agriculture while it also dealt with problems of animal disease. Although the Department of Agriculture and Technical Instruction may not have been as successful as had been desired, it was, at least, a beginning in the establishment of a modern agricultural industry.[9]

Plunkett was not the only member of the ascendancy at this time with an interest in improving the general standard of living in Ireland and solving old problems. In a letter to the newspapers on the second of September 1902, Captain John Shawe-Taylor, a nephew of Lady Gregory, called on named representatives of landlords and tenants to meet in the hope of settling the long running dispute between them. The following December, O'Brien, Redmond, T. W. Russell and T.C. Harrington as representatives of the tenants met with the Earls of Dunraven and Mayo, Colonel Hutcheson-Poe and Colonel Nugent-Everard representing the landlords. Their discussions formed the basis of the Wyndham Land Act 1903.

Encouraged by the success of their attempt to end the land struggle, O'Brien, Dunraven and other members of the land conference examined the possibility of solving other contentious problems by negotiation, most notably the establishment of a university for Catholics. However this policy of 'conference plus business' as O Brien called it was to end in failure. When Dunraven with the aid of Sir Anthony Mac Donnell, an Irish Roman Catholic who was Under-Secretary at Dublin Castle, drew up a document calling for extended powers for local government in Ireland the Unionists became suspicious. They saw it, especially with Mac Donnell's involvement, as a surrender to Home Rule. There were fears among nationalists that negotiations of this type would undermine the Home Rule movement and many of them were unhappy with some of the terms of the Wyndham Act. These criticisms prompted O'Brien to resign from the Parliamentary Party and though he and Dunraven continued to examine the possibility of solving problems by negotiation they were largely voices in the wilderness.

However the whole conciliation movement, limited though it may have been in influence and mass-appeal represented an alternative to the then widely accepted poles in Irish politics, i.e Unionism and Home Rule.[10] This extra parliamentary buoyancy wasn't just confined to economic and socio-political activity. It was also reflected in the growth of what has been called the 'Irish Ireland Movement'.

Throughout the nineteenth century various attempts were made to highlight the wealth of Irish literature and culture, and secure for Ireland her rightful place in the history of western culture. However these attempts were confined to a minority of intellectuals of various nationalities e.g Eugene O'Curry, John O'Donovan, Sir Samuel Ferguson and Jacob Grimm and never remotely achieved the status of mass movements. The Gaelic Athletic Association was the first mass movement to offer Irishmen a feeling of patriotism and pride in games distinctly Irish.[11] It was founded in 1884 by Michael Cusack with the hope of promoting native Irish games to the detriment of foreign games. Its success and mass appeal is reflected in its growth – over fifty thousand members in 1889 – and its influence in restoring pride in Ireland prompted Douglas Hyde to remark in 1892 that the G.A.A. had done more for Ireland in the previous five years than all the speeches of politicians.[12]

Hyde, the son of a Protestant clergyman, with Eoin Mac Neill and Father Eugene O'Growney founded the Gaelic League in 1893 to promote the Irish language and extend its use. However the Gaelic League differed from the G.A.A. in that it was hoped that the League would appeal to men of all origins, creeds and backgrounds. Hyde first won himself a wide audience when in 1892 in a lecture to the National Literary Society he urged Irish men to turn away from things English to things Irish e.g language, customs, manners and literature. This was in essence to be the raison d'etre of the Gaelic League, which by 1906 had nine hundred branches with a total membership of one hundred thousand. With its language classes, magazines, summer schools and festivals the Gaelic League saved the Irish language from being exclusively associated with poverty and backwardness. It also offered to Irishness a cloak of respectability which previously had been in the possession of the foreigner and his clones. Its success can be measured by its achievement in 1909 in having Irish included as a compulsory subject for entry to the newly established National University.[13]

Under the influence of the Gaelic League many smaller literary societies flourished and some of their success is reflected in the establishment by Lady Gregory and W.B. Yeats of the Irish National Theatre in 1897. These societies were mostly confined to towns and at all times were of concern only to a minority. However with the "Irish Ireland" atmosphere that was manifesting itself at the time, the enthusiasm surrounding the 1798 celebrations, the general feeling of support for the Boers in their struggle with the Empire and the stagnation of the parliamentary party it is of little surprise that members of societies such as the Oliver Bond Society of Dublin and the Celtic Literary Societies of Dublin and Cork began to look at political traditions owing more to Wolfe Tone and the Fenians than to Butt and Parnell.[14]

One of the stronger personalities involved in these societies was Arthur Griffith. Born in 1871, Griffith had trained as a printer and was a Parnell supporter.[15] Indeed, he accompanied Parnell to Broadstone Station as Parnell departed to address his last election meeting at Creggs.[16] He emigrated to South Africa at the end of 1896 and returned to Dublin in October 1898. On his return he edited the 'United Irishman', a reasonably successful weekly newspaper. Although a quiet reserved man he could be very critical of colleagues and quite difficult to work with.[17] On the outbreak of the Boer War Griffith started the Transvaal Committee so as to organise public sympathy for the Boers. This committee also helped to equip and dispatch an ambulance corps for South Africa though it was hoped on arrival the volunteers would become more actively involved on behalf of the Boers.[18]

In March 1900 Griffith called for a loose federation of all advanced nationalist societies in the 'United Irishman'. The following September delegates from several literary and political societies met in the rooms of the Celtic Literary Society. A new organisation, Cumann na nGaedhael, following closely Griffith's projections, was suggested. A programme embodying support for the Irish language, arts and pastimes was agreed upon. It also encouraged the protection and development of Irish industries and the development of an Irish foreign policy – the foundations of Sinn Féin policy were being laid. However, even at this stage, the influence of the Irish Republican Brotherhood may be seen as John O'Leary the old Fenian was elected president; the vice presidents elected were Robert Johnson, another old Fenian, and Major John Mc Bride while Griffith himself was almost certainly, at this stage, a member of the Brotherhood.[19] At the Cumann na nGaedhael convention in October 1902 Griffith outlined what was later known as the Sinn Féin policy. The significance of this speech was not appreciated for about eighteen months.

In 1899 Michael Davitt resigned from the Commons as a protest against the British policy in South Africa and also because of the Irish party's hopelessness in parliament. Griffith nominated Major John Mc Bride to contest the vacancy in South Mayo to show the Irish attitude to the Boer War. It was hoped that he would be unopposed as it was probable that on election he would be disqualified, at which time the Irish Party could secure the election of whomsoever they chose. However the U.I.L. selected John O' Donnell, a paid organiser with the League to oppose him. Following a bitter election campaign Mac Bride was soundly beaten, receiving only four hundred and twenty seven votes. [20]

In 1903 following the announcement that King Edward VIII was to visit Ireland a National Council was formed to organise protests. It attracted a range of members from the eccentric Edward Martyn to old Fenians such as John Daly of Limerick and Dr. Mark Ryan of London who saw it as a way to promote the separatist ideal. The National Council was successful in persuading Dublin Corporation not to present a loyal address and it continued as a forum for nationalists to discuss policies and problems. It was opposed to British Government in Ireland and while hoping to assist nationalist representation on elected bodies it also had a programme of progressive social reforms aimed at the abolition of slums and monopolies and the general reduction of taxation. It did not offer a challenge to the Parliamentary party nor did it demonstrate a desire to fight national elections The main emphasis of its programme was on local affairs.[21]

Between January 1904 and February 1905 a series of articles known as the Resurrection of Hungary was published in Griffith's newspaper the "United Irishman". These articles outlined the policy successfully pursued by Franz Deak the Hungarian patriot, who had organised the abstention of Hungarian representatives from the Imperial Diet at Vienna in order to secure the re-establishment of a separate Hungarian parliament in Budapest. The establishment of two separate parliaments linked by the emperor seemed to Griffith to offer an important parallel for Anglo-Irish relations. At the time Griffith did not envisage himself leading a campaign for the adoption of this policy but hoped that some parliamentarians would see the logic of the plan and withdraw from Westminister. Such a policy had already been considered by O'Connell in 1843, by Davis in 1844 and in Patrick Ford's 'New Irish World' in 1876. The policy implied support for a constitution similar to that of 1782 when Ireland had legislative independence.[22]

At the convention of the National Council in November 1905 Griffith outlined a policy for the future. His speech referred to the need for development and protection of home industries and called for the creation of a Council of Three Hundred composed of MPs who would abstain from Westminister along with representatives from local authorities. Máire Butler, a well known Gaelic Leaguer – and a cousin of Sir Edward Carson – gave the name 'Sinn Féin' to the policy.[23] It was also decided to form branches in the country with combative intentions against other parties; this in essence meant the emergence of a new nationalist political party. Peculiarly enough, Griffith himself favoured a propagandist body which would educate by press and pamphlet rather than a political party.[24]

Among the nationalist societies attached to the National Council were the Dungannon Clubs, founded in 1905 by Bulmer Hobson and Denis Mc Cullough, both members of the I.R.B. Séan Mac Diarmada was employed by these clubs as an organiser and though separatist in intent the Dungannon Clubs were not secret organisations. Hobson was elected a non-resident member of the National Executive of the National Council in September 1906 at the second annual convention.

Indeed it may be said that Hobson's membership of the National Council contrasted sharply with that of other members in that for him the 1782 constitution was an unsuitable compromise while for others eg. John Sweetman and Edward Martyn it was the preferred solution. In February 1907 Hobson visited America and was reasonably successful in gathering support but was refused financial aid until unity among the diverse nationalist groups – the Dungannon Clubs, Cumann na nGaedhael and the National Council – was achieved. [25]

In April 1907 at a meeting in Dundalk the Dungannon Clubs and Cumann na nGaedhael amalgamated to form the Sinn Féin League with "regaining the sovereign independence of Ireland" as its objective.[26] P.T. Daly was elected president and it was hoped to contest seats at local and general elections. [27] The Griffith controlled National Council joined the Sinn Féin League in 1907 to form a body that became known simply as Sinn Féin. [28] While some in the new organisation favoured the re-establishment of the 1782 constitution – there were others who would settle for nothing less than total separation. However they were all united by a desire to re-establish the independence of Ireland.

"I have always been of the opinion that this Sinn Féin business is a very serious matter and it has been spreading for the past year. But if the party and movement keep on right lines it will not become very formidable because it has no one with any brains to lead it", commented John Dillon in 1906.[29] This would suggest that the general feeling in the parliamentary party was an awareness of a more advanced movement than that represented by the Redmondites. The electoral success of those advocating Sinn Féin policy would seem to endorse those views. In the Dublin Municipal elections of January 1905 four out of eight Sinn Féin candidates were returned; in the Poor Law elections thirteen candidates were successful, while three out of every four Sinn Féin candidates were returned at the county and District elections in June of that year. In January 1906 Sinn Féin won fourteen seats in the Dublin Corporation.[30]

In the January 4th 1908 edition of 'Sinn Féin' Griffith claimed 25% of the people supported Sinn Féin.[31] However all these figures and claims give a distorted view of the reality. It is most likely that Sinn Féin only fought elections where they had a reasonable chance of success and at this time the parliamentary party showed little interest in local elections.[32] Indeed if the Sinn Féin movement was as widely accepted as Griffith claimed Dillon could be expected to sound a lot more alarmist than he did. In general most people, particularly in rural Ireland were disciples of Redmond and his party.

And so despite the relative buoyancy of advanced nationalism it was largely a united Irish party with considerable support at home that greeted the Sir Henry Campbell-Bannerman led Liberals in Westminister following their victory in the January 1906 general election. Most Irish people felt that the return of the Liberals would bring to an end what amounted to a unionist veto on Home Rule. However they were mistaken. The Liberals were no longer dependent on Irish support following their landslide victory and indeed some Liberals such as Lord Rosebery were opposed to the concept. This resulted in a very watered down type of Home Rule in the Irish Council Bill of 1907. The Council would have control over eight departments of the Irish administration including education, local government and Plunkett's Department of Agriculture and Technical Instruction. The problem was that although some members of the Council were to be elected and others nominated, the Lord Lieutenant had the power of veto which meant that ultimate power still rested with Westminister. [33]

After over ten years waiting for the return of a Liberal government the bill was a major disappointment. In Westminster Redmond was reluctant to absolutely reject the Bill but at home it was totally condemned. Inevitably the feeling of frustration many people felt was bound inspire a more emotional reaction from others. In fact, it led to the resignation from parliament of James O'Mara, M.P for South Kilkenny and the resignation from the party of C.J. Dolan M.P for North Leitrim.[34]

Chapter One

Abroad there is a lady fair, Miss Freedom is her name,
The Harbinger of Liberty, the faculty of fame,
Monarchs all admire her, she dwells in France and Spain,
The foster sister of a youth, called Charley Óg Sinn Féin.

CHARLES J DOLAN

Charles Joseph Dolan was born in August 1881, the son of John Dolan a general merchant in Manorhamilton, County Leitrim and his wife Bridget Fitzpatrick. He received his primary education at a local private school and his secondary education at Saint Patrick's College, Cavan – where he won a gold medal in the Irish Intermediate Examinations. On leaving St. Patrick's he went to

Maynooth to study for the priesthood but finding that he did not have a vocation he left three years later in June 1901, with a degree in Licentiate Philosophy. He later studied at Royal University Wren's, London.[1] By 1908, the family business–now managed by Charles– was struggling.[2] In February 1906, having been proposed by Fr Charles Flynn and seconded by Martin Devaney Co.C. he was selected unanimously by a convention of North Leitrim United Irish League to contest the election caused by the resignation of P.A. Mc Hugh. Mc Hugh, who was the owner of the locally influential 'Sligo Champion', had also been elected to represent North Sligo in the general election in January of that year. Dolan was subsequently returned unopposed –as Mc Hugh had been in the general election.

When he was selected by the North Leitrim U.I.L. Dolan stated that it was his intention to adopt wholeheartedly the policy of the Irish Parliamentary Party. He also referred to the need for Irish children to learn the Irish language and to be familiar with Irish literature and history.[3] This sympathy with the Irish Ireland movement of the time is in stark contrast to John Dillon, a future colleague of Dolan in Westminister who –in 1909 – objected to Irish being a compulsory subject for entry to the National University of Ireland. Dolan's brother James, was a member of the I.R.B., an organisation which would have had few sympathisers in the ranks of the Irish Parliamentary Party.[4] Dolan himself, when speaking at Pettigo in late May 1907, stated that he regretted that Ireland was not strong enough to fight England in the field as the Boers had done.This could be considered extreme language for a parliamentarian, even though at the time frustration was rife due to the limitations of the Irish Councils Bill.

A Member of Parliament who did have sympathies with the advanced nationalists of the time was Dolan's colleague James O'Mara M.P. for South Kilkenny. Born in 1873 O'Mara had first been elected to parliament in October 1900. He had subsequently been re-elected unopposed in January 1906. That he had sympathies with the advanced nationalists of the time is illustrated by his reply to a question concerning Ireland's possible adoption of the Hungarian policy. He asserted that in Parliament the dice was loaded against the Irish members and if the people of the country and the members of the Party felt their attendance at Westminister was no longer useful and that it would be better to try to build a nation at home he would not be the last to agree.[5]

When Birrell introduced his Irish Councils Bill in May 1907 Redmond though disappointed, initially voted with the government.[6] However the official party policy on the bill was to be decided at the National Convention in Dublin on the 20th June.

On the 15th of June, O'Mara, feeling that the English Parliament was no suitable ground on which to fight Ireland's battles, set in motion the process which resulted in his leaving Westminster permanently.*

At a meeting of the North Leitrim executive of the U.I.L. in St. Clare's Hall, Manorhamilton on Sunday16th June a lively discussion took place regarding the advantages of the Irish Party continuing to attend Westminster. Dolan, the Chairman, put before the meeting a resolution which in essence was the Sinn Féin policy, in that it called on the parliamentarians to withdraw from Westminster and campaign for the promotion of Irish industry.

F.E. Meehan Co.C. wondered what the Irish Party could achieve outside the House of Commons. He also pointed to what the Irish Party had achieved in the past and felt that the people should not dictate to the Irish Party. In a later contribution he stated that such a matter should not be considered until after the forthcoming meeting of the National Directory. Laurence Mc Gowan wondered how successful such a policy might be, given the country's meagre industrial resources.

Dolan felt that the National Directory and the Parliamentary Party should be aware of the peoples' feelings before making a decision. He went on that in his opinion the Irish people were as far from the management of their own affairs as they were in O'Connell's time. He felt that implementation of the resolution would ultimately succeed in improving the position of the Irish

* He was not to take an active part in public life until 1918 when he was returned as a Sinn Féin candidate and he was appointed trustee of all Dáil Éireann funds with De Valera and Rev. Doctor Fogarty, Bishop of Killaloe. In November 1919 he went to America to help De Valera raise funds for the Sinn Féin government.

people. He added that he himself had made arrangements to start a boot factory in Manorhamilton and if this project was successful it might encourage others to undertake similar projects. He emphasised the advantages of self reliance and cordial co-operation.

Terence Rooney D.C. felt that the population was decreasing and that employment would introduce prosperity. James Lynott D.C. agreed with Dolan and Rooney and proposed the adoption of Dolan's resolution. Philip Clancy seconded this proposal.

F.E. Meehan commented that while admiring the patriotism of the chairman, Dolan, he himself felt the present move was a rash one. He proposed "that we await the decision of the National Directory as to the line of policy to be adopted for the country." Mr Mulvey seconded this proposal. After further discussion Lynott's proposal – an endorsement of Sinn Féin policy – was supported by twenty seven of the forty one men present. Dolan was selected to represent North Leitrim at the National Convention.

At the convention on the following Thursday, the Kerry M.P. Thomas O'Donnell proposed the following motion – "That after the betrayal of Irish hopes and demands by Mr Birrell's Irish Council Bill, we feel that the Irish Party could do better work for Ireland and make foreign government more difficult, if not impossible by devoting their energy and their talents to the work of rebuilding, extending and protecting Ireland's industries, of fostering the National Language, of acting as guides in land sales, of helping the labourer and town tenant; and we call upon them to withdraw from an assembly which neither legally nor morally has a right to make laws for Ireland, and to initiate at home in Ireland an active campaign of constructive work combined with open and defiant hostility to all English interference in our internal affairs."

This motion was supported by only three delegates: Dolan of North Leitrim, Dr. Mulcahy of South Leitrim the North Longford representative William Ganly. O'Donnell then proposed that in the interests of unity in the commons the nationalist members disaffected with the Irish Parliamentary Party – William O'Brien and Tim Healy – be invited to rejoin the Parliamentary Party. This proposal received some support from southern representatives but was also easily defeated. Although officially the call to re-admit O'Brien was defeated, there still existed a strong feeling at grassroots level in favour of re-admitting him and his followers to the Party. Eventually in November 1907, O'Brien put forward a basis for agreement between himself and the Party. O'Brien, Healy and others finally re-entered the party in January 1908.[7]

On June 21st, the day following the National Convention, C.J. Dolan wrote to Sir Thomas Esmonde, senior whip of the Irish Party, a letter of resignation from the Party. Having referred to the hopelessness and frustration he felt in attending Westminster and the need to adopt a policy of withdrawal Dolan went on to express his regret at leaving the party and his admiration for its members. He concluded the letter:

"As the North Leitrim Executive of the United Irish League has expressed approval of my views I do not intend to resign my seat. As long as I enjoy the confidence of my constituents I shall not turn my back on them".[8]

Predictably Dolan's failure to resign his seat was bitterly condemned by the Parliamentarians. Referring to the pledge signed by Dolan at the time of his selection as a candidate for Parliament to sit, act and vote with the Irish Party, the Freeman's Journal accused Dolan of having a code of honour of his own and doubted if the party to which he proposed to transfer his allegiance would "welcome the proprietor of this elastic code of obligation". McHugh's 'Sligo Champion' did not doubt Dolan's honour, honesty or integrity but opposed

"root and branch the new fangled policy of which he has constituted himself the champion, and which he is endeavouring, at the instigation of a handful of Dublin cranks to foist on the grey beards and veteran fighters of North Leitrim".

It criticised Dolan for not seeking the advice of the Very Rev, The Vicar General of Manorhamilton* and the Very Rev Charles

---

* The Vicar General of Manorhamilton was Charles Dolan's uncle, Rev. James Dolan, a former president of St. Patrick's College, Cavan.

Flynn who acted as his political sponsor in 1905. In North Leitrim various branches of the U.I.L. pledged loyalty to the Irish Party and criticised Dolan for the adoption of his new policy. Typical of of these was the motion passed by Creevelea branch on the proposal of J. Gallagher D.C. and seconded by J. Sweeney:–

"That this committee approve of the resolutions passed at the last meeting of the Directory and pledge ourselves to support them by every means in our power and we entirely condemn the new policy adopted by a few delegates as utterly worthless and deserving of universal condemnation."

Dolan's reaction to this criticism was to announce his intention of resigning his seat, even though he felt that the motion passed by the North Leitrim Executive of the U.I.L., on June 16th demanding the withdrawal of the I.P.P. from Westminster had freed him from the pledge to sit, act and vote with the Irish party. This announcement was welcomed by the Parliamentarians and Redmond stated that he intended to attend the convention to be held in Manorhamilton for selection of a nationalist candidate in the election.

However Dolan's attitude to the I.P.P. and the alternative policies he had adopted were not universally condemned. The unionist 'Impartial Reporter' and 'Farmer's Journal' published in Enniskillen referred to his honesty, intelligence and energy and commented that if Sinn Féin would abandon its insane crusade against England many unionists could join with them, as it was also their wish to build up industrial Ireland, albeit as part of the United Kingdom. As might be expected, the reaction of "the handful of Dublin cranks" had more in common with that displayed by the 'Impartial Reporter' than by the mainstream nationalists. 'Sinn Féin', the newspaper, referred to Parnell's and O'Connell's campaigns outside Parliament and thus the legitimate heirs of these two figures were Dolan and those whom he had joined. In appealing for £500 to take on the vast organisation of the "Irish Whigs" who had a daily press and a vast treasury of £30,000. 'Sinn Féin' compared themselves to Biggar and Parnell when they were attacked by the I.P.P. and the 'Freeman's Journal'.

Chapter Two

Grattan sought and found her and brought her back again
To make the land more happy and to help her to remain,
But villains sold her to the foe for titles and champagne
Which leaves the true heart bleeding of Charly Óg Sinn Féin.

Dolan and his supporters now set about educating the people of North Leitrim in the policies of Sinn Féin. This took the form of organising branches of the Sinn Féin National Council and publishing a newspaper, known as the 'Leitrim Guardian'. The extent of this task can be appreciated by reference to the nature of the constituency. It was a rural constituency, very much in the grip of the U.I.L. – at the North Leitrim Executive meeting held on June 16th which had approved the motion calling on the members of the I.P.P. to withdraw from Westminster eleven branches were represented. Within days of announcing his resignation from the party many of them had assembled to criticise Dolan and to pledge loyalty to the I.P.P. and Redmond. The Ancient Order of Hibernians* was also opposed to Dolan.[1] The Hibernians were superbly organised under the leadership of their Grand Master, Joseph Devlin and were acknowledged experts at getting out the vote at election time.

Compared to these organisations Dolan, and the propagators of the policy to which he was now allied were underdogs. Arthur Griffith himself had calculated that prior to Dolan's resignation there were only six people in the constituency who understood the Sinn Féin policy.[2] The Gaelic League, whose members although politically independent would have been expected to be in sympathy with Sinn Féin had only three branches in North Leitrim.[3] The last occasion on which an election had been contested in the con-

*By 1909 the A.O.H had about 60,000 members

stituency saw the I.P.P. candidate, P.A. Mc Hugh, defeat the Unionist representative, Joseph Singleton, by 4625 votes to 383.[4]

As if these handicaps were not enough, Dolan and his supporters also had to contend with the tradition of parliamentarianism. In 1907 the Home Rule movement, started by Isaac Butt, was about forty years old and it was expecting a lot for people in a poverty stricken rural constituency, such as North Leitrim to abandon it for what was really still a novelty. Cumann na nGaedhal, the organisation to which Griffith had first outlined the Hungarian/Sinn Féin policy he had adapted for Ireland, had only been formed in 1900. Having considered all these disadvantages it is not surprising that Griffith, despite his public statements, commented that if Dolan got one thousand votes it could be considered a victory.[5] Griffith's feelings would have been endorsed by John Keaveney, an organiser of the U.I.L., who visited North Leitrim at the request of the National Directory. Keaveney felt that most of Leitrim had absolute confidence in the I.P.P. and the U.I.L. and that Dolan wouldn't get fifty nationalist votes in an election.[6] However Dolan set about the task enthusiastically and he was ably assisted in the months that followed by prominent members of the Sinn Féin League and the National Council, the two main organisations in the summer of 1907 that were encouraging withdrawal from Westminster and the promotion of Irish industry.

One of the first gatherings in North Leitrim following Dolan's announcement of his intention to resign his seat was an A.O.H. meeting on the fairgreen in Manorhamilton on June 29th. The town was decorated with banners proclaiming messages such as "Ireland Shall Be Free" and "Faith And Fatherland" while branches of the Hibernians from Sligo, Cavan and Leitrim were represented in a crowd of over six thousand. Dolan, Mc Hugh and David Sheehy M.P. addressed the gathering. F.E. Meehan, who acted as chairman, was first to speak and called for a strong united party to agitate for and to foster and develop Irish industries.

Opening his contribution Dolan referred to his pointless attendance at Westminster and apologised for failing to get Home Rule. Ireland, he claimed, could not win at Westminster. He described the I.P.P.'s recently adopted policy of organising mass meetings as a step backwards to O'Connell's time, when it had failed and when it had been ridiculed in England. He wondered what the British Government cared about resolutions passed on the fairgreen in Manorhamilton demanding Home Rule. He concluded by maintaining loyalty to the A.O.H. whose policy he claimed was at one with that of Sinn Féin which he defended by quoting Joseph Biggar – "No Irish Bills but stop English Bills".

In his address Mc Hugh ridiculed Sinn Fein policy. "Mr. Dolan does not ask you to put him in to fight. He wants you to put him in to go and sit down," commented Mc Hugh. Edward Martyn, a leading Sinn Féiner, was also criticised, reference being made to his being a landlord. In Mc Hugh's opinion Tories, Unionists and Anti-Home Rulers would vote for Dolan. He felt there was no need for Redmond to visit the constituency as disunity would be as easily crushed as a fly. He also quoted James Lynott as saying that if he had known his resolution at the North Leitrim Executive U.I.L. meeting on June 16th would be used against the I.P.P. he would have cut off his hand rather than propose it. David Sheehy, in his contribution, referred to various acts passed to Ireland's advantage as I.P.P. successes.

The 'Sinn Fein' report on this meeting was especially interested in the Mc Hugh contribution. His speech was described as a painful surprise to all who heard it and in making no attempt at argument he showed his wisdom. In defence of Edward Martyn it was alleged that in selling his own lands Redmond had charged his tenants twenty seven and a half years purchase while those on Martyn's estates were charged seventeen years purchase. Indeed so disgusted were some people at the meeting that the Manorhamilton band refused to escort Mc Hugh to the railway station – assembling instead in front of Dolan's residence where Dolan, Fr. Terence Connolly C.C.(Manorhamilton) and Bernard McGriskin addressed an enthusiastic gathering. Dolan and his supporters now concentrated their efforts on meetings organised by themselves, with varying degrees of success. On being introduced in Drumshanbo by Fr. Fallon C.C he criticised the I.P.P. and claimed the support of the students in Maynooth. However a proposal from John Moran censuring Dolan and supporting the I.P.P. was opposed by less than a handful of people, including a police pensioner. The 'Freeman's Journal' carried a report that the Newbridge Branch of the U.I.L. had endorsed the demand calling for the Irish members to leave Westminster, but this was later denied.

A meeting of Sinn Féin supporters was held in St Clare's Hall Manorhamilton on Monday July 1st. which, it was claimed, was attended by about two hundred people. A vote of confidence was passed in Dolan who addressed the meeting.

The Belfast born I.R.B. member Bulmer Hobson, one of the most active promoters of Sinn Féin, was one of the first national figures to speak in North Leitrim on Dolan's behalf. Having been introduced to a large market day crowd in Manorhamilton, Hobson explained the Sinn Féin policy. However when he called on the people to demand the withdrawal of the Irish Party from the House of Commons there was some dissent and hostile interruptions. James Lynott then got up on the platform and condemned Dolan for shielding his policy and action behind the North Leitrim executive of the U.I.L. and went on to describe Dolan as "an unmanly and cowardly man." Predictably this was resented, and a scuffle ensued, resulting in the platform being stormed. Dolan and Hobson were manhandled by the crowd and the police had to escort both to the safety of Dolan's premises, which they did not leave while a patrol stayed nearby until peace and quiet were restored. This incident merited mention in the English press where it was described under headings such as *"An M.P. Assaulted"* and *"M.P. Under Police Protection"*. *

Hobson himself was described by Mc Hugh's 'Sligo Champion' as an Orangeman who had been hunted out of America when he went there on the same message of vilification of the U.I.L. and faction mongering as had brought him to Manorhamilton. The 'Champion' concluded by commenting that Dolan's association with Hobson would be as injurious to him as

---

* Dolan's own version of this meeting contrasts sharply with the newspaper accounts. In a letter to O'Mara written a week after the incidents described above Dolan denied being kicked and thumped by an angry crowd, as had been reported and he added that the only one so treated was a man who tried to force his way onto the platform .

the patronage extended to him in his present antics by Rev. Terence Connolly C.C. "whose factionist record is known to every elector in the country. "

In late June – early July speculation was beginning with regard to who might represent the U.I.L.in the forthcoming election. McHugh, John Muldoon and Mr Donovan, who had recently been involved in a dispute over selection in Monaghan, were mentioned as possible candidates. It would appear that Redmond favoured John Muldoon, a barrister at law. He had McHugh investigate the possiblity of having Muldoon put forward in Leitrim. Mc Hugh enlisted the aid of Fr. Flynn who said he would do what he could to have Muldoon selected at the convention. F.E. Meehan, "an able and intelligent shopkeeper" according to Mr McHugh   stated that he would support Muldoon since it was Redmond's wish to have him in the Party.[7]✥ Predictably the National Council nominated Dolan as the Sinn Féin candidate.

In early July Griffith began publishing his addresses to the men of Leitrim in 'Sinn Féin'. These were generally to take the form of endorsing Sinn Féin policy and highlighting various attempts made at promoting it by heroes of the past, while criticising the I.P.P. and its policy. In the first of these addresses Griffith commented that in years to come people would be amazed that at one time it was believed that Irish independence and Irish property could be secured by acknowledging the right of a country, inimical to both of them, to make laws for Ireland and by sending eighty men to fight five hundred and seventy men under the conditions chosen by the five hundred and seventy.

John Redmond, speaking at Battersea in early July said that the Sinn Féin policy of withdrawal had been rejected by every Irish leader since Grattan. He wondered what would happen to the development of Irish industries and the tenants if their only representatives in Westminster were the Orangemen of the North. He continued that in times of crisis cranks came to the surface and that the new policy was simply an old one– destroy the Irish National Party. However, it is probable that comments such as

---

✥ Muldoon was subsequently chosen by the U.I.L. in Wicklow to contest an election on their behalf.

these reflect a certain amount of frustration and annoyance with Dolan which are not in keeping with McHugh's expressed confidence at the recent A.O.H. meeting in Manorhamilton and the usual contempt expressed for Sinn Féin by Parliamentarians. Redmond's statement that —

> *"Upon how the present political situation in Ireland develops depends whether the present National Movement will continue to advance by slow, perhaps, but steady steps towards triumph, or whether it will go back into the melting pot and disappear for our time into chaos and confusion."* [8] –

reflected Griffith's view that North Leitrim had the opportunity to identify two distinct groups in Ireland: those who believed in the right of the British government to govern and those who believed the contrary. [9]

Further evidence of this nationwide U.I.L. resentment of Dolan and of the proposal for an alternative to parliamentarianism are the regular references made to both by parliamentarians throughout the country in the summer and autumn of 1907. They were regularly referred to at those meetings, which were organised as part of the campaign to boost the traditionalists' morale following the disappointment of Birrell's Irish Council Bill. For example John O' Dowd M.P. claimed that Dolan wanted to pose as a greater man than Redmond in his attempt to force a faction fight in North Leitrim and Samuel Young M.P. stated that Ireland was too dependent on the English market for the isolationist policy of Sinn Féin to work.

In North Leitrim itself the U.I.L. and A.O.H. continued to display loyalty to Redmond and his party while at the same time showing their disapproval of Dolan. On Sunday, July 6th meetings were held at Drumkeerin, Newbridge, Kilenummery, Creevelea, Killasnett and Glencar at which new members were welcomed, loyalty was sworn to Redmond and the I.P.P., and Dolan was roundly criticised – "as he has betrayed his constituents in an unpardonable manner and we will never recognise a Sinn Féiner in our midst". Indeed at the Kilenummery meeting evidence was given of Dolan having visited the parish the previous day only to be accosted by Charles Meehan, a member of the committee, who informed the visitor that they were ashamed of him and had called for three cheers for Mr. Redmond and the Irish Party.

However, that Dolan's campaign had now gained momentum is illustrated by his visiting Killenummery and Drumkeerin. He had also addressed enthusiastic gatherings at Newbridge, Glenfarne and Kiltyclogher. By mid July arrangements were well advanced for the publication of his newspaper while the nation-wide appeal for funds had also achieved some success.

Griffith's latest appeal to the men of Leitrim pointed out how parliamentarianism had failed Ireland by referring to how tillage acreage and population had decreased. At the same time the number of people in poor law unions, the poor law rate per head and taxation had all increased. Consideration was also given to the establishment of a University which had been promised in 1871 but was still being debated in 1907. Parliamentarianism had resulted in the inadequate 'Irish Councils Bill'. 'Sinn Féin' also criticised the 'Freeman's Journal' for reporting violence in North Leitrim – the market day incident in Manorhamilton involving Dolan, Hobson and Lynott – while failing to condemn its promoters. Dolan's new found popularity with the advanced nationalists is illustrated by the endorsements he received from the Sinn Féin oriented National Council. Branches in Dundalk, Blarney and Castlebar were among those who congratulated him – some of them hoped to be seeing the end of parliamentarianism while mere mention of his name at a meeting in Tuam was greeted by applause.

Undoubtedly Dolan gained exposure for those promoting an alternative to attendance at Westminster. This resulted in him speaking to meetings at Enniscorthy and Dublin. How Dolan himself felt at this stage is best illustrated in a letter he wrote to O'Mara about this time. While expressing optimism he acknowledged the disadvantage of the people not being familiar with the Sinn Féin policy and the need for political figures of real significance to be seen endorsing his position.

*"I would intend to resign very soon but I want to
have as much time as possible to educate the people.
They are coming round and I believe we shall win. Up
to the present the only help I have had is from boys and
the people want to see men of standing connected with
us."*

This is a tacit admission that he had failed to convert a substantial
part of the U.I.L. establishment - leaders at a local level, thus
ensuring an uphill struggle, despite his optimism. He concluded
with an oblique reference to the parliamentarian view of him
while also expressing the effect the latest developments in his
political life were having on him personally.

*"I am busy night and day and would give anything for
a week's rest. The strain of this thing is awful but no rest
for the wicked and erring parliamentarian."* [10]

In general the clergy throughout the constituency adopted a
reasonably low profile in regard to the difference of opinion
among the nationalists. With the exception of a few– eg. Fr.
Connolly, Dolan got little support from the clergy – most of them
being happy to endorse the I.P.P. Indeed Keaveney the U.I.L.
organiser, claimed he had met no priest in the constituency who
supported Dolan. In Killargue Rev. Charles Flynn expressed disapproval of the do nothing policy and also referred to the achieve-
ments brought about by the I.P.P. In early July the Bishop of
Kilmore, Dr. Boylan, endorsed the I.P.P. policy and encouraged
all Irishmen to support the U.I.L.That this endorsement was
advantageous to the parliamentarians is shown by the welcome it
received from Manorhamilton Branch of the U.I.L.,who while
declaring their confidence in Redmond and the party, called for a
rejection of factionism and announced their pride in and gratitude
to Dr. Boylan. This endorsement of Dr. Boylan's may have influenced Dolan's uncle the Vicar General, who was conspicuous,
throughout the campaign, by his silence.

The U.I.L. in Kinlough and Rossinver was re-organised and
promptly joined the other branches throughout the constituency in
proclaiming loyalty to the I.P.P. and condemning factionism.

Further evidence of the difficulties being experienced by Dolan was the reception he was given by the people at the Manor Chapel after mass on a Sunday in mid-July. Having been introduced to the crowd by Fr. O'Keefe C.C. only one man – John Gilroy who was employed by Dolan – remained to hear the new apostle of faction. However, July was also to see what could have proved to be a major boost to Dolan and nationally to the Sinn Féin movement, while simultaneously undermining the nationwide confidence in the I.P.P.

THE NEW "OLD MAN OF THE SEA."

"I am convinced that Parliamentary agitation, as now conducted, has spent its force, and that nothing more can be gained by it on its present lines." . . . . . "I do not believe that the English-speaking people will ever grant Home Rule or anything like it."

Letter from SIR THOMAS ESMONDE, M.P.—*Daily Papers*. July 22nd, 1907.

Chapter Three

But her ladyship is coming for she is too long away
Sycophants and critics are the cause of her delay.
But when she comes with fifes and drums, we'll tell the world
  plain
That we wish success to her sweet self and Charley Óg Sinn
  Féin

On July 19th the London correspondent of the 'Freeman's Journal' reported that he had recently been told that Sir Thomas Esmonde a senior member of the I.P.P., had informed Redmond that he was out of sympathy with some of the party's policies and wished to resign. He subsequently resigned his post as whip of the Irish Party at Westminister and intimated his intention to resign as a Member of Parliament and of the national organisation.

At a Sinn Féin meeting on Sunday, July 21st. in Enniscorthy a letter from Esmonde was read in which he said that Parliamentary agitation as now conducted was a spent force. Esmonde's public criticism of the party and his resignation as whip were significant in that he held an important position in the party and was one of its senior members. Originally both O'Mara and Dolan had hoped that Esmonde would resign with them and that others could be persuaded to do likewise– and so strengthen the abstensionist policy.[1] At the Enniscorthy meeting, which was also addressed by Alderman Walter Cole, Alderman Seán T. O'Kelly and Griffith, Dolan reiterated the frustration he had experienced in his fifteen months at Westminster and also claimed that while he did not advocate physical force he would not stand in the way of the Irish people if they were ever prosperous and strong enough to appeal to arms.

His presence at the Enniscorthy meeting prevented Dolan from attending a meeting of the North Leitrim Executive U.I.L.

However a letter apologising for and explaining his absence was read to the meeting. He also intimated that he did not wish to be re-elected chairman of the Executive. However the meeting objected to the reading of a letter from Esmonde as those present were not interested in the views of a factionist. Fr. Flynn said that the chairman of the meeeting, F.E.Meehan had stood by the executive at the critical time and "had saved the situation".

One of the first contributions to the meeting, during which some Sinn Féin supporters outside kept up a din, came from James Lynott who stated that although he did not like differing with Fr.Flynn he felt he had to clear the air as he sensed innuendo in Flynn's remarks regarding "saving the situation." Lynott went on to explain that he had proposed the resolution – demanding withdrawal of the I.P.P. from Westminister – passed at the meeting on 16th June at Dolan's request. The resolution had been drafted by Dolan and he, Lynott, recognised the citizen's right to make the proposal. However he also recognised the right of the Irish Party to reject the proposal and had he known of Dolan's relations with the party or had he thought Dolan would use the resolution to leave the party he would never have supported it as he would be the last person to assist faction in Leitrim. Meehan endorsed what Lynott said and went on to claim that he himself had declined Dolan's request to propose the resolution.

There is no reason to doubt this version of events as on 29th of May, at least two weeks before the original meeting to discuss the Irish Council's Bill, Dolan had written to O'Mara: –

"I have been thinking about what you say regarding our future policy and, though I fully agree with the force of your arguments in favour of obstruction in the House of Commons, I feel too strongly on the subject of withdrawal to reconcile myself to returning. As you know, I took a long time to make up my mind as to the wisdom of the Sinn Féin policy, but once having come to a decision, there is no going back. I do not intend to return to Westminister but I want you to keep this secret from everyone for a few weeks." [2]

This correspondence suggests that the two men had worked

together for some time in regard to working out a policy which, at the very least, contrasted with the conventional I.P.P. policy of campaigning at Parliament. More importantly a full two weeks before the North Leitrim Executive of the U.I.L. had demanded the withdrawal of the I.P.P. from Westminister Dolan had taken a unilateral decision not to return there and therefore his manipulation of the delegates at the North Leitrim Executive meeting was only a means of justifying his resignation from the party.

Needless to say at their meeting of July 21st the North Leitrim Executive rescinded the motion, which had demanded implementation of the Sinn Féin policy, and went on to vote confidence in and support for the Irish party led by Redmond. Calls were also made on Dolan to resign his seat – which some delegates felt he would have done if he had any honour left in him. Some delegates expressed sympathy with Dolan– on account of his father who had been an active member of the U.I.L. up to the time of his death. Fr. Flynn was surprised that an intelligent man had adopted such an impractical policy. He felt Dolan must have doubted the intelligence and patriotism of North Leitrim and when given the chance to express their views the voters would do so in most emphatic and unmistakable way.

Evidence of a recent visit to Ballaghmeehan by one of Dolan's organisers, Mr Daly, was given by Mr McPartland – representing the Rossinver branch. When Dolan's supporter was asked what he had ever done for Ireland the reply was "nothing", as he had no time and had always to look after himself. When he commented that the I.P.P. was responsible for increased taxation and emigration he was told that Mr McHugh had been responsible for keeping forty five families in their homes on the Tottenham estate. The meeting was assured that Mr Daly got short shrift in Ballaghameehan.

Fr. Flynn proposed Dan Boyle of Manchester as a suitable candidate in the forthcoming election. He stated that Boyle had been born on the borders of County Leitrim and had for thirty years been an ardent supporter of the I.P.P. through devotion of time and money. In his sponsor's opinion Boyle would be a suitable candidate who would represent their views and be a worthy representative. Mc Partland seconded the proposal commenting that he lived near Boyle's birthplace, knew him personally and went on that he was a credit for the service which he had given Ireland. This proposal met with the unanimous approval of the executive who were congratulated by David Sheehy on their unanimity. He went on to describe the Sinn Féin policy as narrow, shallow and ineffective designed to hinder the Irish Party. Replying to criticisms made of the Irish Parliamentary Party John O'Dowd M.P. stated that many present at the meeting could remember their condition before '81 and the improvements they now enjoyed were the answer to this question. He also felt that the I.P.P's policy of fight in the British House of Commons as well as fight on the hillsides of Ireland was the only policy that could effect Ireland's regeneration. It was decided to hold a public demonstration under the auspices of the North Leitrim Executive at Drumkeerin on a date to be arranged.[3]

On the day following the North Leitrim Executive meeting Dolan addressed a public meeting in Dublin. Having referred to his reasons for resigning from the I.P.P. he outlined the difficulties he had to overcome in Leitrim, including Mc Hugh's influence and what he described as "violent misrepresentation in the press". He also announced that since he had already intended appealing to the constituents, he felt that he was no longer bound by the decision of the executive to rescind the motion which had demanded implementation of the Sinn Féin policy. He concluded by stating that he would resign at a time of his own choosing. Dolan and Esmonde were also appointed members of the Central Branch of the National Council of Sinn Féin.[4]

About this time conciliation moves were initiated by some members of the Irish Parliamentary Party, including Thomas O'Donnell. He suggested, at a meeting on July 27th, that a conference of all Nationalist members be held so as to secure National Unity. However the suggestion was overwhelmingly rejected for what appeared to be a very good reason– how could a group that rejected parliamentarianism unite with those who saw it as the only practical solution. Esmonde's decision to apply for the Chiltern Hundreds, the process of resigning from the British

House of Commons was welcomed by this meeting– though his departure was regretted.* The I.P.P. reaction to Esmonde's imminent resignation contrasted sharply with their reaction to Dolan's, since the former had also decided to resign his seat, something Dolan had failed to do despite the encouragement he had received from the U.I.L.and the I.P.P. Though Esmonde's resignation was regretted, the North Wexford U.I.L. condemned his policy and endorsed the I.P.P.[5]

In North Leitrim both Dolan's supporters and those who opposed him continued to promote the policies for which they stood. Efforts to win support for Dolan in Drumshanbo at the end of July met with dismal failure. Andrias O'Broin arrived in the town and his initial attempt to address an after Mass meeting was unsuccessful as no one would introduce him to the crowd. Efforts to educate a market day crowd were equally unsuccessful. Aided by "a gossoon from Glenfarne named Mc Dermott", O'Broin having distributed literature, attempted to address a meeting which had to be abandoned due to heckling from the crowd and both men had to receive R.I.C. protection. [6]

On Sunday 28th July a meeting was held in Manorhamilton to form a branch of the National Council. At the meeting Dolan claimed to have the support of almost all his fellow citizens and that in Manorhamilton the Parliamentarians would not get twelve votes. Resolutions were passed, supporting the policy of self reliance, criticising the Sligo Champion for suggesting that Dolan had to receive police protection –which he denied– condemning the Secretary of the Manorhamilton Branch of the U. I. L for failing to inform committee members of a recent meeting–, a charge he had already denied, and urging the people to support Irish industry. In recognising the failure of Parliamentarianism the meeting decided to form a branch of the National Council.

* The Chiltern Hills are in Oxford, Buckingham and Bedford counties. The area was once infested with robbers on account of which an official named the Steward of the Chiltern Hundreds was appointed by James 1 to protect the people. It is held to be an office of profit under the crown and any member accepting an office of profit under the crown must vacate his seat, subject to re-election. The acceptance of the nominal stewardship of the Chiltern Hundreds by a member who wishes to resign his seat effects his release, simple resignation being illegal. The custom dates from 1750.

Officers elected were C. J. Dolan M.P. President, John Gallen Vice President, Patrick Wilson treasurer, Patrick Fox secretary and Peter O'Reilly assistant Secretary. Dolan had hoped that O'Mara might address this meeting but his former colleague in Westminster could not do so, owing to the death of his brother-in-law. A collection was held that realised £3.14s.6d – Dolan having contributed ten shillings. The national 'Sinn Féin' appeal for funds had by now raised £219.9s.

Griffith continued his addresses to the people of Leitrim and wondered what the I.P.P. had done to encourage the re-opening of the iron mines in Leitrim or industrialisation of any kind. He felt that parliament had reacted to external measures both in 1828 and during the Land War. He went on to say that since the Redmondites were so preoccupied with participation in parliament they would have opposed both these movements. [7]

In early August Dolan intimated his intention to resign his seat when Parliament adjourned and as the election was about important issues and along new lines the people needed plenty of time to make up their minds. In reply the I.P.P. accepted what Dolan said but since an election could not be held during recess it was felt that Dolan should resign before the rising of Parliament which would be inside the next three weeks. The Freeman's Journal expressed frustration with Dolan's continual stalling which, it felt, would upset Sinn Féin's chances.

Evidence of Dolan achieving some success was illustrated by meetings of Glenfarne Branch U.I.L. and Drumkeerin Hibernians. At a meeting of the local U.I.L. in Glenfarne a motion forbidding members to promote Sinn Féin policy received six votes with three against – but significantly seven of those present abstained. At Drumkeerin the local Hibernians decided that henceforth those who supported Sinn Féin policy would be expelled from the order.[8] That either of these motions was even proposed is a tacit admission that some people were sympathetic to Dolan's new policy. Indeed the 'Impartial Reporter' felt that Sinn Féin had won over the majority of the U.I.L.in Glenfarne and Manorhamilton. It also commented that the constituency's seven hundred Unionists would, most likely, support Sinn Féin.

Nationally Esmonde was again stealing the limelight from Dolan. The member for North Wexford withdrew his letter of resignation and, not surprisingly, this decision was welcomed by the Parliamentarians. How enthusiastic Esmonde was about his re-entry to the parliamentary ranks is questionable since as recently as mid July he had written that Parliamentary agitation, as then conducted, was a spent force while in the Autumn he wrote that he believed the future was with Sinn Féin.[9] Indeed his statement at this time that he would support any body of Irishmen pushing the National Rights of Ireland to the forefront does not reflect the sentiments of one whose sympathies were exclusive to the Parliamentarians. It is quite possible that Esmonde renewed his membership of the I.P.P. only in order to avoid an acrimonious split in Wexford such as had occurred in Dolan's constituency.

Meanwhile Redmond accused Dolan of running away from the polls. He also criticized those who accused the party of doing nothing to help Ireland while not appreciating the tiresome work old members of the party had been doing for many years.[10] Redmond also announced his intention to address a meeting in Killargue on the last Sunday in October.

The 'Sligo Champion' quoted articles in the 'New York World' criticising Sinn Féin and Bulmer Hobson. The American publication quoted John O'Callaghan, the Secretary of the U.I.L. of America attacking Sinn "Fakers" who did not accept the English Parliament though contesting English run elections while accepting protection from English police. Hobson "the little Belfast nondescript", had, in O'Callaghan's opinion no right to criticise the I.P.P. as he did not represent any public body. O'Callaghan also ridiculed the lack of Irishness in Hobson's name while in reference to Hobson possibly being of Quaker stock he commented that it was strange to have as leader of a fighting movement one who came from a group whose motto was "peace at any price". Hobson experienced further abuse in mid-August in Newry when a meeting he was chairing had to be abandoned because of heckling and violence.[11]

While on the national stage Esmonde's re-entry to the parliamentarian ranks was a set back, the emergence of John M Parnell,

Charles Stewart's brother, as a Sinn Féin supporter could be seen as a boost. In a letter to the 'Irish Independent' Parnell wrote that the I.P.P. were incapable of developing Ireland financially or commercially. While he may have had an axe to grind with the parliamentarians, his support lent credibility to Sinn Féin's and Dolan's claims to be the legitimate successors of Charles S. Parnell.

August also saw Dolan visiting the northern end of the constituency. In Kinlough he stated that he wasn't forcing his views on the people but rather outlining his reasons for leaving Westminister and the advantages of a new National Policy.[12] Predictably the Tullaghan Branch of the U.I.L. felt Dolan would be better employed fighting the battle of the poor evicted tenants rather than putting Irishmen against Irishmen.[13]

Griffith continued to highlight the foolishness of the I.P.P.'s attendance at Parliament. He claimed that since 1871 the number of paupers in Ireland had doubled while the population had fallen by one million. He also illustrated the cost of bureaucracy to Ireland– of every pound spent by the poor rate only 10s 6d actually went to the relief of the poor, the remaining 9s 6d was spent permitting the relief to reach them.

At a meeting of Sinn Féin supporters in Manorhamilton, chaired by Thomas Gilgunn in the absence of Dolan, arrangements were made to hold meetings and distribute literature. On addressing a gathering in Glenfarne, Dolan himself stated that nothing could be secured by talk and since armed resistance couldn't be used passive resistance should be employed. Confirming Glenfarne's interest in Sinn Féin, on the proposal of John Mc Loughlin–Vice President of the Cloonclare U.I.L. – a branch of the National Council was established with Mr Brennan D.C. as president, the other officers being with a few exceptions the same as those who had comprised Cloonclare Branch of the U.I.L. Dolan was also cordially received by a meeting in Lower Glenfarne chaired by Ben Maguire later that day. There Dolan said that great men preferred deeds to words and claimed that Parnell had never boasted about what he and his party had accomplished. He concluded that national independence was necessary for Ireland and could only be won by an active and determined policy of self reliance. A resolution to form a branch of the National Council was passed unanimously.[14] At a subsequent U.I.L. meeting in Glenfarne Keaveney– the U.I.L. organiser – was well received by "veteran nationalists". At this meeting John McGowan D.C. stated that although Dolan had appointed him treasurer of the National Council branch, he had done so without his – Mc Gowan's– consent and he had publicly protested against the use of his name in such a cause.This meeting also decided to expel "cranks" i.e Sinn Féin supporters at the next U.I.L. meeting.[15]

Speaking in Killasnett a week after visiting Glenfarne Dolan stated that he did not want politics to cause ill feeling between any neighbours. He felt that every man should have his own opinion while respecting that of his neighbour. He concluded by stating that a man who attempted to create faction by listening to none but his own political opinion was Ireland's enemy. A branch of the National Council was also formed with the following elected: Jas McDonald, President; John Mitchell, Lisnabrack, vice-President; William Mc Sharry, Russaun, Treasurer; James Rooney, Lecknarainey, Secretary; and James O'Donnell, Glebe, Assistant Secretary.[16] However speaking at Killasnett Branch of the U.I.L. Fr. McGovern C.C. stated that no one with common sense would support Dolan's policy and he called on the people to stick to the U.I.L. policy that had won concessions over the previous twenty five years. Following an address by Keaveney at Mullies it was also decided to expel Sinn Féin members from the local U.I.L. branch. Kiltyclogher, Drumkeerin and Newbridge branches of the U.I.L. all passed motions encouraging the purchase of Irish goods, following correspondence from the National Directory – a knee jerk reaction to Sinn Féin perhaps. Other U.I.L. branches continued to pledge loyalty to Redmond while criticising Dolan for failing to resign his seat and causing dissension.[17]

What was possibly one of the most important developments of the North Leitrim campaign was the decision in August 1907 to amalgamate the Sinn Féin League and the National Council – heretofore two independent autonomous organisations.* This new group became popularly known as 'Sinn Féin'.

The officers elected were Edward Martyn, President; John Sweetman and Arthur Griffith Vice–Presidents; Walter Cole and Seán T. O'Kelly, Hon. Secretaries; Councillors O'Carroll and Sheehan Honorary Treasurers.[18] The amalgamation effected the bringing together of those who accepted the notion of a dual monarchy (e.g. Martyn) and those who favoured a truly independent Ireland (e.g. Hobson). Almost the only thing they had in common was frustration with the I.P.P. – a frustration to which Dolan gave expression.

* For the background of both organisations see Introduction.

Chapter Four

Arise ye sons of Erin at home and o'er the wave,
Your country it lies bleeding, will you not strive to save
The dear old land that gave you birth and blood to every vein
And God will bless our noble work neath the banner of Sinn Féin

Moving into mid September, Dolan's supporters were making an impact throughout the constituency on behalf of Sinn Féin, branches had been organised in several places, and almost £580 had been collected to conduct the campaign. It was also reported that a propaganda campaign was about to be inaugurated in London beginning with a demonstration likely to be addressed by, among others, the Member of Parliament for North Leitrim.[1] The fledgling branches of the National Council now set about projecting Dolan as a hero, where heretofore he had ben projected as a villain by the U.I.L.

At the Manorhamilton Branch Committee meeting of the National Council delegates were selected to attend National Convention and there was unanimous approval at the amalgamation of the Sinn Féin League and the National Council. At Glenfarne the following motion was passed:–

" That we record our entire confidence in Mr C.J.
Dolan and call on his constituents to give him the sup-
port he honestly deserves, in his manly stand for
National Independence, which we believe can only be
won by the policy of Sinn Féin and self-reliance."

That Dolan was achieving some success, at least in establishing the importance of supporting Irish industry is illustrated by a warning given by the Manorhamilton branch of the National Council to the public to be wary of hawkers selling foreign produce as Irish manufacture. At a later meeting– when it was also decided to call the branch the John Mitchell Branch– a committee was appointed to organise the distribution of posters, to be printed locally by 'The Leitrim Guardian', advertising the gravity of this matter. Young men were also encouraged to ignore a recruiting

P.A. McHUGH

sergeant in the area as any recruit could be considered "an enemy to the sod which bore him". Evidence was also heard of how a paid U.I.L.organiser – Keaveney– was visiting areas after Dolan and imploring the people not to listen to him.

On one occasion anticipating that Keaveney would visit Cloonclare a supporter of Dolan's – Seán Mac Diarmada – went there and on his arrival the U.I.L. organiser found his meeting being addressed by Mac Diarmada. When he was invited to debate the issues involved Keaveney refused – describing the Sinn Féiners as blackguards and tramps. He also ignored a challenge to show any Irish garment he was wearing.[2] This meeting was described by the 'Sligo Champion' as an effort to re-organise the League and it claimed that despite the best efforts of Sinn Féin to disturb the meeting, a strong working party was established. However even the Champion had to obliquely concede that in Glenfarne Dolan was converting some U.I.L. supporters in that it reported that J. Keaney and James Feeney had been elected to succeed Philip Clancy and Philip Maguire as secretary and assistant – secretary, both having previously being won over by Dolan. Further evidence of converts to the Sinn Féin Policy was the decision of the Manorhamilton branch of the U.I.L. on the 6th of October to expel committee members identified with "the stay at home policy".[3]

The 'Leitrim Guardian' was now in use as a a medium by which Sinn Féin supporters could criticise the I.P.P. as led by Redmond while demonstrating that their own policies were more constructive and in keeping with the traditions of Parnell. The new paper felt that the Irish Party had no policy, instead that it drifted with the tide waiting on something to turn up while basking in the glory of resolutions of confidence. It went on to illustrate how obstructionism and holding the balance of power were the two main features of Parnell's policy. Rule changes in the House of Commons had rendered obstructionism out of order while Redmond, by delivering the Irish vote in England to the Liberals had ensured that they had become strong enough to abandon Home Rule. Parnell's policy commented the Guardian, was no longer practicable – the only thing to do was take the advice he had given in 1882 and boycott the Commons. *"The Irish Party has no policy. They are trading on the reputation of Parnell, and are tolerated for the sake of the past. To express confidence in the policy of the Party, is absurd, as it is expressing confidence in something which does not exist,"* commented the' Guardian' – expressing much of what was wrong with the parliamentarians in the minds of many advanced nationalists at the time.[4]

Speaking at a meeting in the Mansion House in September, Redmond appeared to concede that little had changed since the 1880s when he stated that the modern Irish Party was the same as in Parnell's time. In emphasising that Home Rule was the only way of reviving industry he was, perhaps, acknowledging that at least some of the Sinn Féin suggestions were constructive. A further concession was his admission that armed resistance "would be absolutely justifiable if it were possible."[5] This was emotive language for someone who was later to be described as one who found it hard to hate Englishmen, and was even to encourage Irishmen to fight with Britain in the Great War. However it is not unreasonable to suppose that the sentiments expressed in 1907 may have been prompted by some Sinn Féin supporters outside the building who prevented some Redmondites from entering the meeting.

October 27th saw Redmond address the U.I.L.'s largest gathering in North Leitrim and greatest show of strength throughout the campaign. Prior to the meeting, held in Drumkeerin, Dolan arrived accompanied by Fathers Galligan (Dromahair), McLaughlin (Glangevlin) and Kelly (Newbridge). Newbridge was acknowledged to be a Sinn Féin stronghold. However the Redmondites had the bulk of clerical support present and letters from Dr. Boylan, Bishop of Kilmore and some parish priests calling for unity in the nationalist ranks i.e. endorsing the U.I.L. were read to the meeting. The speakers, who included Dan Boyle, referred to the need to support Irish industry and the need for a united Party. He also cited I.P.P. successes down the years. Redmond having thanked the gathering for their confidence in him, stated that a good organisation was necessary at home as it encouraged the party in Westminster. Dolan, who smiled whenever he was mentioned, was in Redmond's opinion an able young man whom he had thought had a great career in front of him. He respected Dolan's right to change his opinion but criticised him for declining to "give his constituency an opportunity of saying whether the people approved his action in leaving the Irish Party, and it is at the Polls alone that such proof could be ascertained".

At the end of the meeting Dolan made an effort to address the gathering but was greeted with groans, boos and calls of "No Faction here," "Clear out" and "traitor". When he persisted the crowd became angrier and some mud and stones were thrown. The crowd dispersed only after the police intervened following appeals from some of the clergy. It may appear that Dolan was foolish to expect a hearing at this gathering or that he was simply goading his rivals. However it is quite probable that the crowd's reaction was not as spontaneous as it seemed* On his arrival home in Manorhamilton Dolan was met by the local band and he addressed an enthusiastic gathering. He described how he had

*See Appendix III re letter to locals to have crowd "worked up".

46

been refused a hearing by a lot of ignorant yahoos, even after several priests had appealed for order. He went on to challenge either McHugh or Redmond to debate the relative advantages of both policies at a Sinn Féin demonstration the following Friday in Manorhamilton. An 'Irish Times' report of this gathering prompted a vitriolic reply from the 'Sligo Champion'. The 'Champion' wondered why intelligent people would listen to the "drivel and hogwash mouthed forth by Castle clerks and Dublin corner boys." Dismissing the challenge to debate it commented that Dolan, on whom most people looked with feelings of disgust and pity, should know that Redmond wouldn't touch him with a forty foot pole. It also felt that it was the electorate and not arguments that would decide the issue.[6]

The Drumkeerin gathering was followed some days later by a large demonstration in Kiltyclogher organised by the local U.I.L. Enthusiastic groups from all the neighbouring districts attended while banners declaring 'HOME RULE', "IRELAND A NATION" and "UNITED WE STAND" spanned the streets and evergreens and bannerets adorned the platform. Again motions demanding Dolan's resignation and declaring loyalty to Redmond and the I.P.P. were passed. The speakers, included John O'Dowd M.P. and Dan Boyle who had travelled overnight from Manchester to be present. Indeed on his arrival at Glenfarne Boyle had been met by bands from Belcoo, Kiltyclogher, Rossinver and Derrygonnelly. The platfrom party accused Sinn Féin of waiting until the bulk of the work had been done before offering themselves to the people. The meeting looked forward to the defeat of the new policy being promoted by a few irresponsible non-entities.[7]

The Sinn Féin meeting in Manorhamilton of the following Friday was attended by a crowd estimated at one hundred (Sligo Champion) and over two thousand (Sinn Féin). 'The Champion' claimed it was a fiasco attended mainly by conservative game keepers, landlord hangers on and the curious while Glenfarne and Killea were the only country districts represented. Not surprisingly the Sinn Féin report viewed the proceedings more favourably. The town was thronged from an early hour and decorated with arches bearing mottos such as "NO LONDON PARLIAMENT".

The meeting, chaired by Felix Rooney D.C., began with the passing of resolutions which criticised the participation of Irish members in the British House of Commons, called on the people to support Irish industries, expressed confidence in and support for Dolan and demanded the formation of a National Council in Dublin.

Andrias Ó Broin addressed the meeting in Irish and English. Apparently many in the crowd understood the Irish language. Dolan, in his speech, referred to the futility of attendance at Westminster where most members were hostile to Ireland. Indeed Irish representatives had little influence and when they spoke, it was to empty benches as the English members had walked out. Referring to Redmond's speech in Drumkeerin Dolan noted that his former leader had made no statement with regard to his, Redmond's, future policy. This was not surprising since he had no policy, parliamentarianism being a spent force. Dolan went on that in 1905 Redmond had said the Irish Party would only support the Liberals if Home Rule was promised. The support had been given but Home Rule was as far away as ever. He then offered the Leitrim Election Fund, which amounted to in excess of £500, as a contribution to the establishment of a Leitrim industry – provided the Parliamentarians would contribute a similar sum. He then proposed that the election be fought out publicly and legally with returning officers chosen by the people at comparatively little cost. He would abide by the result and if the parliamentarian candidate secured a majority he would permit him to be officially returned unopposed.

Griffith wondered if the people would strike down the man who had come home and admitted that the Irish members had been fooled and betrayed. Paraphrasing Parnell's "Keep a firm grip on your homesteads" he urged the people to "Keep a firm grip on your country". Having referred to the emigrant ship, the workhouse and the paupers grave he illustrated the livelihoods which Ireland's resources would support. He concluded by urging the people to make the Leitrim Election the Clare Election of National Self Government. Mr. J O'Flaherty D.C., Loughrea repudiated the I.P.P. claim that Sinn Féiners were mushroom politicians.

He described the present policy of the parliamentarians as "faked public meetings which had no meaning except to humbug and which led nowhere". In conclusion he stated that he would go all over Ireland to support Dolan, whom he described as a true and manly Irishman who had risked everything to let his constituents and countrymen know the truth. Cllr. P.T. Daly described the Parliamentarians as Whigs masquerading as Home Rulers while Séan MacDiarmada asked the people when had they heard so much commonsense spoken to them from a public platform. He stated that the future depended on work, not talk and he concluded by appealing to the people to return home sober– the spirit of Sinn Féin being self respect.

Dolan's offer to hold a plebiscite was lauded by Sinn Féin which pointed out that it could make available up to £600 for industrial development in North Leitrim. Initially it was ignored by the Parliamentarians, as was an address given in New York by a former Leitrim M.P. Michael Conway. In it Conway supported withdrawal from Westminster and argued that if the Irish members worked in conjunction with the public bodies at home the situation in Ireland would be revolutionised.[8]

Four months had now passed since the North Leitrim Executive of the U.I.L. had passed the motion demanding the withdrawal of the Irish Party from Westminster. In that time Dolan had resigned from the party and had made a big effort to educate the constituency as to the logic of his new policy. He had achieved moderate success and doubtless he had exposed the "Hungarian Policy" to a far wider audience than it had heretofore experienced. Whatever apprehensions the founding fathers of the Sinn Féin movement may have had about contesting the election they gave him great support, For nationalists frustrated with parliamentarianism he was a source of inspiration– one described him as "a young man of whom any organisation might be proud, who had sacrificed money, prospects and even friends"[9] However he had been the only Member of Parliament to resign and wholeheartedly campaign for the Sinn Féin policy. This must have been a source of disappointment for both Dolan himself and his Dublin mentors.

In contrast it is probably fair to say that for the

Parliamentarians the situation was nationally an irritant and locally an embarrassment. For a movement which had enjoyed practically an unopposed monopoly of nationalist support for forty years these developments were very frustrating. With the exception of the end of the Parnell era few difficulties had been encountered and they had met no nationalist opposition in almost any form since their formation. Given these circumstances and the potential long term threat offered by Sinn Féin the vitriol which Dolan, Griffith etc. encountered is understandable. Neither is it surprising that in mid-October the Impartial Reporter commented that despite the activity of Sinn Féin the U.I.L. still had the support of the clergy and were in control of the constituency. Dolan was aware of this and by this time must have been pessimistic — otherwise he'd have long since resigned.

The Leitrim Guardian

Vol. 1. No. 31.]　　MANORHAMILTON, SATURDAY, FEBRUARY 29, 1908.　　[Price One Penny.

EXTRACTS

FROM THE

SPEECHES

DANIEL O'CONNELL,

As Published in the "Stare Trial."

"We are governed by foreigners ... Ireland ... in what it calls the Imperial Parliament ... "

D. O'Connell at the Royal Exchange, Dublin, 1810.

"An Act of Parliament ..."

D. O'Connell's Speech in the delivery of 1843.

"Fellow-countrymen, we consider by calling upon the Irish to re-establish that the old ..."

THE FIGHT ON THE "FLOOR"

IRELAND'S WEAPONS

(Continued.)

Chapter Five

I'm Francis Meehan, the people's choice, a candidate for
  Parliament
I'll tell you now what I'm goin' to do, if to the House I'm sent.
I'll order King Ned give ye all Home Rule and then with your
  consent
Every house in the land will be painted green, if I go to
  Parliament.

Following the two major rallies in Drumkeerin and
Manorhamilton, November and December saw few developments
in the campaign. U.I.L. branches continued to criticise Dolan and
to endorse the I.P.P. In mid- November the Central Branch of the
National Council heard that eight branches of the National
Council of Sinn Féin had been formed in North Leitrim. Séan
McDiarmada was confident that branches could be formed in districts originally hostile to Dolan. Up to sixty members had
enrolled in the Kinlough branch which had been formed following
a large meeting addressed by Dolan and MacDiarmada. 'Sinn
Féin' felt this reflected the change in North Leitrim in the previous months as many of those who had joined in Kinlough were
extremely opposed to Dolan when he had first visited the area following his adoption of the Sinn Féin policy.[1]

'Sinn Féin' of November 30th castigated the lack of development in Ireland and in Leitrim particularly during the time Irish
members attended Westminster. It predicted that if the population
continued to fall at its present rate there would be nobody living
in Leitrim by 1942. It then examined what constituted "industrial
Leitrim" and commented that there was not enough industrial
work to sustain a town of five acres let alone an Irish county of
390,000 acres.

On December 3rd. Dolan wrote to Redmond outlining the
advantages of a plebiscite, as proposed at the Manorhamilton

meeting, and how it might be organised. Redmond acknowledged Dolan's letter, out of personal courtesy, but he refused to consider the proposal seriously. The 'Sligo Champion' was more explicit in rejecting Dolan's offer. It commented that there was nothing to ensure Dolan would accept the result of an unofficial election if he were defeated and went on that Dolan's election fund – now more than £605 – was given to him for faction mongering and this was what he should use it for. It also wondered why Dolan would contest an election to a parliament in which he did not intend participating.[2] Redmond's rejection of the plebiscite subsequently prompted a Castleisland supporter of Sinn Féin to call on Dolan to refuse to contest the election on parliamentarian conditions and ignore the Irish party as they – the parliamentarians – were refusing to contest the election on Sinn Féin conditions.[3]

In mid-December the Manorhamilton Branch of the U.I.L. felt that public meetings should be held to protect the nationalists of North Leitrim against the invasion of the Little Hungarian Band. It was decided to invite Messrs. Kettle , Devlin and Hazelton to address a monster demonstration to be held in Manorhamilton at an early date.[4] That the U.I.L. should feel it necessary to do so was, perhaps an admission that it was the Sinn Féin campaign which had most momentum at this stage. This is not surprising since Sinn Féin could only improve their standing– compared to what it was in June – while the U.I.L. had everything to lose. The attendance of national figures at demonstrations could at best improve morale and restore the U.I.L. to their previous position of unchallenged authority.[5]

End of year reviews in both camps differed in their observations on recent developments. Sinn Féin had seen the number of their followers increase nationally, with a significant strengthening of support in North Leitrim. They looked forward to a general election in 1908 which they hoped to contest in twenty counties. In forthcoming Dublin Municipal elections eight wards would feature Sinn Féin candidates. The year concluded with a meeting of the eleven branches of the National Council which had by now been formed in North Leitrim. Each branch was represented by four delegates and the main discussion centered on Dolan's possible resignation. Some of the delegates felt Sinn Féin would be disgraced if Dolan did not resign but eventually it was decided that he should not yet do so. Dolan was satisfied to leave the occasion of his resignation in the hands of the committee and the authorities would be informed when it was felt the time was right.

In contrast, at a meeting of the local U.I.L. in Killargue, Fr Charles Flynn P.P. accused Dolan and "his little Hungarian band of faction mongers" of insulting the clergy and intelligent men of North Leitrim. He accused Dolan of "living in a Fool's paradise" and claimed that all Irishmen supported North Leitrim in the movement for the country's regeneration. Many of the traditionalists felt Sinn Féin had no chance of victory and nowhere is this better illustrated than Killargue. There, due perhaps to the influence of Fr.Flynn, the local U.I.L. were able to congratulate themselves "that no Sinn Féiner ever dares show his nose in this historic parish".[6]

In the Dublin municipal elections on January 3rd. four Sinn Féin candidates were returned and they had a combined vote of 6,751. There was disappointment however in the failure of prominent Sinn Féin spokesman Walter Cole to retain his seat. The size of the support may have encouraged Sinn Féin supporters. However these votes were cast in a municipal election and there was no guarantee that they would be repeated in a parliamentary election. The U.I.L. in Dublin did not place too much emphasis on local elections and more importantly, it would not be unreasonable to expect the city of Dublin to be more favourably disposed to a non-traditionalist policy than North Leitrim.[8] Given these circumstances the size of the Sinn Féin vote would hardly have boosted Dolan's confidence.

Nationally January was significant for the Parliamentarians as William O'Brien and his supporters re-entered the Irish Party at Westminster.[9] Although having little influence on the situation in North Leitrim this development would have improved morale in the parliamentarian ranks. It also meant that, with the exception of Dolan, all the nationalist members of parliament were united, temporarily at least.

At a meeting of the John Mitchell Branch of the National

Council in mid-January Dolan intimated that he wished to resign his seat. He requested the Secretary of the Committee of the North Leitrim Branches to summon a meeting so that his resignation could be forwarded to the proper quarter and preparations might be made for the forthcoming election.[10] He accused Redmond of rejecting an opportunity for Irish men to run Irish affairs by his refusal to have a plebiscite. In defence of his own withdrawal from Westminster Dolan quoted Parnell: "If the constitutional movement were to fail I would not continue one hour at Westminster". He described the forthcoming election as an opportunity for the people to declare that Ireland was not a subject province but an independent nation.[11] The 'Sligo Champion' commented that Dolan had broken his pledges so often that at this stage nobody could take his word. It went on to state that Redmond would hold no further communication with Dolan.

A further effort was made to establish Sinn Féin in Drumshanbo on Sunday January 19th. On that date MacDiarmada and Lynch attempted to speak at the chapel gate but were forced by the crowd to withdraw to High St. However the arrival of John Moran, a leading U.I.L. figure in the area, prompted the Sinn Féin representatives to run to their hotel. An angry crowd calling "We'll tear them to pieces" and "No runaway policy for us", attempted to gain entry to the hotel resulting in police intervention. The 'Sligo Champion" accused MacDiarmada and Lynch of trying to deceive Moran, whom they dreaded, by advertising that their meeting would take place in Kiltubrid. Then on the day before the meeting, in his (Moran's) wife's name, they wired him to come immediately to Carrick. On his arrival in Carrick, Moran realised that the call was a hoax and returned to Drumshanbo. This incident, six months after his resignation from the Irish Party – illustrates Dolan's lack of support and progress in some areas of the constituency.

On the following Sunday, January 26th, a meeting of the North Leitrim Committee of the National Council took place. There was some disagreement about Dolan's future tactics— some delegates even suggesting that he should rejoin the Irish Party. Eventually it was decided that he would resign on getting instructions from the Central Executive.[12] This resulted in Dolan sending his application for the Stewardship of the Chiltern Hundreds i.e. his resignation to Captain Donelan Senior Whip of the I.P.P. two days later. On receipt of the application Donelan submitted it to the Chancellor of the Exchequer. On Wednesday, February 5th Donelan moved the writ for the election of a member to represent North Leitrim and on the following day the speaker's warrant for the holding of an election arrived in the Crown and Hanaper Office in Dublin.[13] Owing to the death of the High Sheriff, Captain Darley of Carrick-on-Shannon it was felt the election might be delayed. However it was subsequently decided that it would take place on February 21st. with nominations being accepted on February 14th.[14]

The local U.I.L. responded to these developments by advertising a meeting of the North Leitrim Executive for Sunday February 9th. Subsequently this meeting was cancelled when it was decided that the parliamentarian candidate in the election would be selected at a convention in Drumkeerin on Tuesday, February 11th.

This was contrary to a request from the Manorhamilton U.I.L. that the Convention be held in Manorhamilton as it had the best facilities and was the most accessible and central venue.[15] Sinn Féin viewed the decision to hold the convention in Drumkeerin as an admission of their strength in Manorhamilton. P.A. McHugh was nominated to take charge of the parliamentarian campaign, having done likewise – according to 'Sinn Fein' – in the 1890 election against Parnell.[16]

Predictably Dolan was selected to represent Sinn Féin in the forthcoming election. This was the signal for Sinn Féin to launch an offensive on his behalf. Sean O'Riadaigh secretary of the Castleisland Branch of the National Council appealed for further contributions to the election fund as he feared that if it amounted to less than £1000 it would be proof that those who believed in Dolan's policy were not in earnest. It was confidently predicted that Sinn Féiners would travel from all over the country to North Leitrim to work on Dolan's behalf while appeals were also made for automobiles to be placed at the disposal of the National

Council.

'Sinn Féin' commented that the traditionalists were ridiculous and illogical in criticising laws passed by the British Parliament as it was their presence in Westminster that gave the House of Commons the authority to rule Ireland. The Parliamentarians, and those who voted for them, were described as Unionists since they were recognising the Act of Union as being lawful and binding. It was the opinion of Dolan's political sponsors that the election offered the first opportunity for Ireland since 1805 to demonstrate that the British Parliament was not the legislature for Ireland. It pointed out that Hungary's experience with Austria, and Finland's with Russia, were proof that the strongest empire in the world had no resource against the weakest nation refusing to acknowledge its government except the Dragoon.* As a result of refusing to recognise the Emperor of Austria as King of Hungary the Hungarians were now free and among Europe's most prosperous nations. In contrast Ireland was enslaved and was also civilisation's poorest and most wretched country.

Irish representation in the House of Commons had according to Sinn Féin, resulted in three insurrections, four general famines, twenty seven partial famines, thirteen great industries extinguished, the abolition of the Irish exchequer and Custom House, a fivefold increase in the taxation of Ireland, a twenty-five percent reduction in the population, the emigration of five million people and the conversion to pasture of eighty percent of the country's tillage land. Objections to these developments resulted in imprisonment: and Parliamentarianism– far from stopping this plunder and oppression had made it legal. The Irish presence in Westminster had degraded Ireland morally and materially and reduced it from a nation to a province. The Parliamentarians had meant well but all they could do was make rhetorical speeches while the people perished and were plundered of seventy million pounds. Parnell had said he would give parliamentarianism a trial and if it failed he would return to Ireland. Parliamentarianism had failed but his successors would not consider another policy.

* In 1907 following years of Russian dominance the Finns had succeeded in establishing a Parliament – of restricted importance – elected by universal suffrage.

Emphasising the role the North Leitrim By-Election would play in replacing the old stagnant policy of parliamentarianism 'Sinn Féin' predicted that ten years after the election the most respected men in Ireland would be those who had voted for Dolan. It also claimed that "in a free Ireland, men will boast of their descent from the voters of Leitrim who in 1908 broke the fetish before which Ireland had grovelled for generations and cleared the road for the triumph of Sinn Féin."

The need for an Irish Consular Service was highlighted and its establishment would be one of the priorities of the Council of Three Hundred. A Consular Service would ensure that Ireland was neither misrepresented nor maligned. It would develop Ireland's foreign trade which had suffered under Westminster rule to the extent that Ireland had no direct trade with many European countries. Representative meetings in Dublin would be concerned with Irish business and not that of the Whigs and Tories.

In an eve of poll address Dolan referred to the idealism with which he had entered the House of Commons and the reality that had greeted him. Any confidence he had in the Liberals was destroyed by the Irish Councils Bill and he felt that if he had continued to attend Westminster he would be deceiving his constituents and betraying the cause of Irish nationalism. It was his experience that England was not interested in Ireland and that appealing to English men was demoralising and a waste of energy. He outlined Ireland's decay over the previous fifty years and claimed that it was action in Ireland that would remedy the situation. The establishment of an Irish Council in Dublin – as contemplated by O'Connell– could look after Ireland's industrial, agricultural and financial interests. It would encourage wealthy Irishmen to invest their money in the development of Irish industry and illustrate the advantages of using Irish products. Commenting on a possible suppression of an Irish Council Dolan claimed there was nothing to stop representatives of the Irish people meeting in Dublin and forming a Parliament. If re-elected he would assist in the establishment of the council and as representative of the area he would attend to the needs of North Leitrim and the development of its industrial resources. He would direct the attention of the Irish in America to Leitrim's great mineral wealth and its potential for employment. He would endeavour to obtain American assistance for the establishment of industries. Ireland did not need the assistance of any English party but rather the service of all her sons, Catholic and Protestant, and he was willing "to co-operate with Irishmen of all creeds and causes in advancing the interests of our common motherland." Dolan claimed to stand for a free, prosperous, self-reliant Ireland and he concluded "I am confident that if you give me your support and loyal co-operation, we shall soon succeed in bringing about a change for the better in the condition of our country. Sinn Féin means the end of empty talk and humbug, and the beginning of genuine National work; it means more wealth, more employment, and better wages for the people; it heralds the dawn of a new era rich with promise for our long suffering country, and as a believer in the policy of Sinn Féin, a believer in a self-reliant, self-supporting Ireland, I confidently solicit your support."[17]

Not surprisingly having tendered his resignation and thus finally precipitated an election Dolan now felt the full fury of the Parliamentarians as expressed by the 'Sligo Champion'. It felt Dolan would get no more than a few hundred votes and that he had reduced his chances of success by not resigning in June or July when there had been a feeling of dissension. The result was a foregone conclusion and Dolan was called on not to force an election. Referring to their failure to contest recent parliamentary vacancies it wondered did Sinn Féin think Leitrim was the best place to look for "political fools". Dolan had been selected by castle clerks under the presidency of a landlord and he would get the votes of orangemen, rent office hacks and political outcasts. He had broken the trust of the men of North Leitrim who had elected him when he had no political experience but since joining Sinn Féin Dolan seemed to have an unrealistic idea of his own importance and that of his constituent's character and intelligence. It predicted that any votes Dolan got would not be for his policy and would give pleasure to the country's enemies and lower his status in the constituency.[18]

'Sinn Féin' reacted to accusations of this sort by illustrating that it was not just Dolan's supporters who had connections with the British establishment. It reported that in late January McHugh had been nominated for membership of the British National Liberal Club. A condition of membership of the B.N.L.C. was that the applicant describe himself as a 'Liberal' and that his sponsor endorse this description. It was claimed that though fulfiling these conditions McHugh, and his colleague for South Sligo J.O'Dowd, had responded to this revelation by withdrawing their applications – until the completion of the North Leitrim election.[19]

The Ancient Order of Hibernians were now promoting F.E. Meehan as a possible candidate for the traditionalists. The St. Clare's Division– Manorhamilton – unanimously passed the following resolution on January 31st. "That we the members of the above division beg to recommend to the electors of North Leitrim the name of our worthy president, Bro. F.E. Meehan, Co. C. as a fit and qualified candidate to represent them at the coming election for a member of Parliament." Similar resolutions were subsequently passed by the Glenade, Glencar and Kilasnett divisions.

Local branches of the UIL also endorsed Meehan as a potential candidate. At a meeting of the Manorhamilton Branch he was described as having served the true cause of nationality with vigour and determination while his intimate knowledge of the problems of North Leitrim's people meant he would not let them stay in the background. Meehan commented that he did not desire such compliments and he did not aspire to such responsible duties. However the attitude and tactics of those creating disension among nationalists meant he would accept the decision of the forthcoming convention.[20]

The Ballinaglera Branch of the U.I.L.expressed dissatisfaction at the decision to cancel the meeting of the North Leitrim Executive U.I.L. which had been arranged for February 9th at Manorhamilton. This dissatisfaction was based on a feeling that Dolan would have responded positively to this call, thus avoiding the expense and turmoil of an election. It was also decided that in the event of the convention refusing to consider asking Dolan to rejoin the party the Ballinglera delegates would take no part in the proceedings.[21]

The U.I.L. convention in Drumkeerin was presided over by Rev. Pat Mc Morrow. It was attended by two hundred and thirteen men. It had been predicted that either F.E. Meehan or Dan Boyle would be selected. Rev. Charles Flynn proposed and P.J. Flynn J.P. Chairman of Carrick R.D.C. seconded Meehan. The convention, which was held in private, unanimously endorsed Meehan's candidature. Following the convention a public meeting was held at which P.A. McHugh described Meehan as a gentleman and the first person to oppose Dolan when he tried to fool the people of North Leitrim. He predicted Dolan would get little support as there were no political lunatics in Leitrim. He felt that the Sinn Féin candidate had reduced his chances of success as the people were sick of dissension and now they had a united party fighting for them. Dolan was accused of having turned his coat and eaten his principles and of asking the people to do likewise. McHugh claimed Dolan had a touch of swelled head which the people knew how to deal with. He went on that Dolan had requested that he be allowed absent himself from Parliament and McHugh felt that the kind men of Leitrim would grant that request.

In his address Meehan, who was enthusiastically received, – thanked the delegates for selecting him as the candidate for "noble historic North Leitrim". Unlike Dolan he could claim neither a college career nor gold medals. However he could boast that he had the confidence of the north Leitrim electors and that he would promote their interests and wants. It was his opinion that Dolan had been manipulated by clever Kildare St. Club politicians but by their actions in Drumkeerin the people of North Leitrim had sounded the death knell of factionism in the constituency. He was proud to join a united party led by the noble Redmond. With regard to industrial development he felt that agriculture was Ireland's most important industry. The people should learn about it and its advancement as factories and foundries would fall and wear out. Meehan was confident of victory and that happiness and would rest upon the land.[22]

Not surprisingly the 'Sligo Champion' reacted positively to the deliberations in Drumkeerin. It told its readers that North Leitrim was a nationalist constituency, not a part of Hungary, and as such it would row in with the rest of the country. Reference was made to Meehan's having been selected by the people and not a few non-entities from Dublin. As a man of quality and experience the parliamentarian candidate was a thousand times more suitable as a representative than Dolan. An attack made by Redmond on Sinn Féin the previous July was quoted and the 'Champion' felt that Dolans' friends would be doing him a disservice if they voted for him. An easy victory for Meehan was the 'Champion's' forecast.

Chapter Six

Corned beef and cabbge will grow high outside each door,
I'll supply strong drink and the weaker kind to the rich and to
*   the poor,*
I'll compel the hens to lay boiled eggs and you'll dine to
*   your hearts content*
And I'll fill the canals with whiskey if I go to Parliament.

FRANCIS EDWARD MEEHAN

Francis Edward Meehan was born in September 1864, the fourth child of Laurence Meehan, a farmer and businessman, and his wife Jane Rooney. He was educated at Manorhamilton Intermediate Classical School and St. Patrick's College Cavan. He was a publican, the proprietor of two shops in Manorhamilton and three farms. His brother was Fr. Joseph Meehan C.C. Dromahair while another brother John –deceased– had at one time paid £15,000 for Glenade estate. He was president of Manorhamilton division of the Ancient Order of Hibernians, the North Leitrim Executive of the United Irish League and the Catholic Young Men's Society. Two years previously Meehan had been co-opted on to Leitrim County Council and he also held a seat on the Leitrim Technical Committee. This near perfect political pedigree was complemented by the possession of a fine physique, and a capital singing voice. He was "interested in all branches of sport while in his younger days he had been a cricketer of more than local repute," according to 'The Impartial Reporter.'

The day following Meehan's selection as the parliamentarian candidate was the fair day in Manorhamilton and a meeting was held on his behalf outside the Market House. The speakers included P.A. McHugh, James Lynott D.C., Thos. McGovern J.P., John Keany and a U.I.L. organiser from Belfast, Dermot O'Brien. In his address McHugh felt that some people might feel obliged to support Dolan as his uncle was the Vicar-General of the Diocese of Kilmore but it was the Sligo M.P.'s opinion that Monsignor Dolan would be supporting the parliamentarian candidate. He went on that the election would be fought out by the free judgement of the electors, not with sticks and stones but warned that if any attempts were made to interfere with the parliamentarians they would know how to wipe the streets of Manorhamilton with their opponents. When Meehan spoke he stated the the people's enthusiasm showed their support for the old methods and that the I.P.P. had won much for Ireland and shouldn't be abandoned. He also felt that the faction mongers would never recover from the blow they would receive in North Leitrim.

While the traditionalists were holding their meeting Dolan addressed a gathering of Sinn Féin supporters—complete with band—from the window of his own house. Having outlined the disadvantages of the parliamentarian policy and criticised McHugh, Dolan turned his attention to Meehan.He had always felt Meehan was a nice quiet man, not interested in politics but he appreciated the amusement he had been given by Meehan's singing of comic songs. The Sinn Féin candidate criticised his opponents for holding a meeting when men were engaged in selling cattle and claimed that this had forced him to address a gathering. He pre-

A THING OF THE PAST.

JOHN REDMOND—"Bad luck to that infernal machine with the foreign name. Ever since
it come on the road I have lost any fares I had. I can't afford to give the poor baste a
feed of oats. I'm to blame meself. Me ould yoke is a bit slow, and it's out of date. I
was wan time in comfortable circumstances."

dicted that Meehan's supporters would be disappointed in expecting the streets to run with blood.

Confirming that this might happen, the police were forced to intervene in several scuffles in the crowd as both meetings were held simultaneously and convenient to each other. Two men were taken into custody but a Sinn Féin supporter who was assaulted refused to prosecute as he did not recognise an English court.

Following his resignation Dolan's first meeting was held in Ballaghnabehy. On a wet, cold day four hundred people and two bands attended and they were addressed by Dolan, McDiarmada, Ben Maguire and P.Clarke. A successful Sinn Féin meeting was also held on the Dowra-Ballinaglera border.

Two days after the Manorhamilton meetings Wilton Vaugh Sub-Sheriff, received nominations on behalf of Francis E. Meehan, Nationalist and C.J. Dolan nominee of the Sinn Féin party. Despite having written from Dublin that he intended contesting the division, Matthew Kennedy did not put in an appearance nor did anybody attend on his behalf. Over fifty nomination papers were handed in on Meehan's behalf while Dolan was nominated by a bailiff, Pat Brennan, who according to the Champion, had only joined Sinn Féin as he failed in a bid to become Chairman of Manorhamilton Board of Guardians.

Having handed in their nominations both candidates adjourned to Kiltyclogher—where a fair was been held. Meehan and his supporters were greeted by the local A.O.H. band. Meehan wondered if the people could have faith in Dolan, a weathercock politician, who had been a member of the Irish Party, A.O.H. and U.I.L. and was now doing his best to cast ridicule on these organisations. Mc Hugh claimed Meehan was far superior to Dolan. He went on that Dolan had requested his support in getting a situation from Horace Plunkett as he had failed in an attempt to get a government post. Normally McHugh would refuse such a request but he was willing to stretch a point for John Dolan's son. Dolan had then mentioned the possibility of representing North Leitrim and Mc Hugh thought he was suitable.* However Dolan had been a complete failure in the Commons. Commenting on a rumour that Glenfarne priest, Fr. McCabe, was supporting Dolan the Sligo

M.P. said that anyone who had dined with Colonel Adamson was too low to advise good people.

While this meeting was in progress Dolan and some of his supporters accompanied by the music of the Glenkeel Fife and Drum Band arrived in Kiltyclogher. This group marched past the parliamentarians and having done so the band gave an energetic performance about thirty yards from the meeting. McHugh demanded that the band stop playing and warned that if the police–who were present–did not intervene then he and his followers would do so themselves. The band ignored this threat and eventually the parliamentarian supporters attacked the Dolanites. Despite the best efforts of the police to keep the opposing factions apart "a battle royal ensued in which fists, feet and sticks were freely used". Hopelessly outnumbered, Dolan's supporters were forced to retreat to safety. Unfortunately, for himself, one of the few who failed to reach sanctuary was the man in charge of the big drum and as it was he who had been largely instrumental in inciting the attack he was suitably punished. The drum itself was destroyed– the ultimate indignity possibly being the sight of a member of the A.O.H. dancing a hornpipe on it. Meehan himself received a blow to the face when he asked a Sinn Féin supporter, whom he caught hold of, to put down a stone. As at Manorhamilton some arrests were made.

Following this musical interlude the meeting resumed despite some minor scuffles. Dolan and MacDiarmada were among the listeners for a brief period. Subsequently they spoke to an assembly of their own supporters and Dolan was able to claim that members of Ballinaglera U.I.L. had signed his nomination paper. He accused the Irish Party of being afraid to upset the Liberal Party. He went on that McHugh was opposed to Sinn Féiners as their policy would put an end to loafing about the lobbies of the House of Commons.

* In an interview with the St.Louis Post dispatch in August 1930 Dolan himself claimed that his father had been chosen as the Nationalist Candidate for the Parliamentary election of 1906. He informed the committee that he could not accept the nomination and Charles was then requested to let his name go forward, which he did.

Compared to these incidents the parliamentarian meeting which was held in Drumshanbo on Saturday 15th February, to coincide with the local fair, was a peaceful affair. With no sign of any Sinn Féin support the Meehanites were given free expression which they used to condemn faction while encouraging support for their candidate. McHugh denied a report in the 'Belfast Telegraph' that Ballinaglera U.I.L. were supporting Dolan and predicted that a parliamentarian meeting to be held there on the following day would be well attended. He went on to accuse one prominent U.I.L. member in Ballinaglera – Mulvey, who was a member of the platform party– of supporting Dolan only because he himself had failed to be nominated and McHugh claimed that he had proof of this. This prompted one man to try to pull Mulvey off the platform but this was resisted by members of the gathering who informed McHugh that Mulvey was as good a man as he. Referring to the support Dolan was getting from some young clergymen out of personal friendship McHugh wondered if faction was being promoted at Maynooth. He accused them of being turncoats and claimed they would have no influence on intelligent men. It was McHugh's opinion that Dolan only joined the Sinn Féin "Funkers" as he was jealous that he wasn't sent on a trip to America with able young men such as Hazleton and Kettle. He went on to predict that Dolan would suffer the same fate at the polls as the big drum had experienced in Kiltyclogher the previous day.

Meehan again outlined the advantages of a united pledge bound party and urged the people to vote, not for him but for the cause which had won them so many concessions in the past. John O'Dowd M.P. claimed many members of Sinn Féin were ex-policemen and ex-government servants and described the election as the dying kick of factionism. In his contribution Peter Cowley Co. C. compared the three F's which the I.P.P. had won to the three F's Dolan was offering – faction, folly and fraud.

There was much activity in the constituency on the Sunday following Meehan's selection as a candidate. Both groups advertised meetings for Glenade. After Mass Dermot O' Brien began addressing the attendance and shortly afterwards Dolan arrived accompanied by helpers from Kerry and Wexford as well as George Gavan Duffy, son of Sir Charles Gavan Duffy. With the majority of the people listening to O'Brien the Sinn Féiners decided to do likewise. O'Brien claimed Dolan had accepted £20 a month salary for being an M.P. though not earning it and he accused him of insulting the people in his "rag of a paper", by saying that they were not self reliant. In his opinion Dolan had not enough supporters to make a respectable funeral for a lady's pet dog. He went on that Sinn Féiners were interested in the Irish language though not two dozen of them understood it while Dolan himself did not understand a word of it. O'Brien also felt the Parliamentary Party stood for Parnell's policy. All of these claims resulted in denials and retorts from Dolan–including one in Irish. The outgoing M.P. claimed he had given up his salary for four months before leaving parliament. He also announced that Parnell's sister Anna would be arriving in the constituency on the following day to canvass for Sinn Féin. Dolan claimed that this was an endorsement of his policy by one well acquainted with Parnell's.

Seán MacDiarmada attempted to speak to an after Mass crowd in Drumkeerin but was unable to make himself heard due to the groans and hisses of the intended audience. Indeed police intervention was necessary and eventually the Sinn Féiners made their way to Strandhill, about three miles from the village, and held a meeting there.

The traditionalists had advertised that a meeting would be held in Ballinaglera on Sunday. However before the candidate arrived a meeting was held at which it was decided that neither Meehan nor anyone speaking on his behalf would be given a hearing. This was primarily because, at the time, the local U.I.L. were involved in a land dispute and they did not wish to actively participate in the election. There was also considerable support for Dolan among senior U.I.L. members in Ballinaglera, some of them having spoken on his behalf. McHugh had further antagonised the people in his treatment of Mulvey – the secretary of the local U.I.L. –the previous day in Drumshanbo when he had tried to turn the crowd on him. McHugh's claim that Mulvey had attempted to gain selection was dismissed by Patrick McGreal. It was pointed that any improvements brought about in Ballinaglera were achieved through the united action of the people with little support from the I.P.P. in the House of Commons.That there was, at least, some antipathy in Ballinaglera towards the national movement is substantiated by a report which claimed that it had been decided unanimously to support Dolan and that seven hundred votes in the district had been pledged to him.[1]

Probably being aware of this resentment to his campaign Meehan anticipated some trouble in Ballinaglera. As a result, on the day previous to the meeting he sent telegrams to various people seeking their support.

O'DONNELL, PRESIDENT A.O.H DRUMKEERIN.
"BRING AS MANY CAR LOADS AS POSSIBLE TO BALLINAGLERA MEETING TOMORROW AT ELEVEN. I PAY EXPENSES.

MEEHAN"

MCDONALD, PRESIDENT A.O.H. BLACKLION
"IF POSSIBLE BRING CONTINGENT TO BALLINAGLERAGH MEETING TOMORROW ELEVEN. I PAY EXPENSES.

MEEHAN"

On their arrival in Ballinaglera it was made clear to McHugh and Meehan that they were not welcome. They were unsuccessful in their attempt to address a meeting and only the intervention of the local U.I.L. committee and police prevented the parliamentarians from being severely abused. A contingent of four cars carrying supporters from Manorhamilton was forced to turn in the Dowra direction although Meehanites from Drumshanbo, Drumkeerin and Newbridge were not interfered with. Subsequently some of Dolan's supporters held a meeting in Ballinaglera while the parliamentarians retreated to Newbridge.

There McHugh acknowledged the right of the Ballinaglera men to make up their own minds but predicted that of the two hundred people likely to vote in Ballinaglera one hundred and seventy five of them would support Meehan. He reaffirmed his feeling that a few men were manipulating the majority of the U.I.L. members in Ballinaglera. He would continue to work on their behalf but the actions of their leaders had isolated the people of Ballinaglera from other branches who could be expected to support them.

'Sinn Féin' complimented the men of Ballinaglera on standing firm and commented that Meehan's offer to pay expenses could be interpreted as payment from the Parliamentary Fund. It wondered would the treasurers of the fund, Stephen O'Mara, Alfred Webb and Bishop O'Donnell sanction use of the fund in this manner. It also stated that following these developments McHugh had instructed Joe Devlin– secretary of the U.I.L. and Grandmaster of the Board of Erin A.O.H.– to send Condon, Hayden and Kilbride to the constituency thus ensuring that "the whole of the available twenty pounders have been turned on the constituency, and the floor of the British House of Commons will miss them for some days to come, whilst they are fighting the battle of British Liberalism at home."

On Monday February 17th a group of parliamentarian representatives consisting of McHugh, Lynott, Hazleton and O'Brien went to Ballaghameehan to address a meeting. In his contribution McHugh related how the parish priest, Father Brady, had been requested to give the village hall to some Sinn Féiners for a meeting. The cleric refused the request – offering instead a stable which he considered more appropriate. While this meeting was in progress a group of Sinn Féin supporters passed by and although both groups abused one another there was no violence as the police maintained a strict line between them. Dolan's supporters proceeded to hold a meeting at which speeches were delivered by MacDiarmada, O'Kelly and Gorey-man, J.R. Etchingham. The parliamentarians enjoyed the spectacle of a lone Sinn Féin flag bearer having to get a police escort while passing their meeting.

In Drumkeerin the arrival of Meehan, O'Dowd and Denis Johnston was followed soon after by that of Dolan, George

Gavan-Duffy and Anna Parnell. The traditionalists were enthusiastically received but eggs, mud and other missiles were thrown at the Sinn Féiners. This prompted the police to intervene and they escorted Dolan and his supporters to an hotel. A police cordon had to be put round the hotel to prevent the crowds approaching it. The traditionalists then held a meeting and subsequently Anna Parnell, followed by Dolan and Gavan Duffy tried to do the same but they were forced back into the hotel. A police cordon had to be put round the hotel to prevent the crowds approached it. Later Parnell made another attempt to address a meeting but the box on which she stood was pulled from under her. She also had a bucket of water thrown on her while Gavan Duffy's silk hat was broken by a stick. Dolan also encountered abuse in this incident in which stones and mud were flying. Following a request from the police sergeant O'Dowd appealed to the crowd after he had been guaranteed that no Sinn Féin meeting would be held. This ensured the Dolanites were subjected to no more violence and were allowed to leave Drumkeerin. Parnell was however more successful in her attempt to speak to Fr Flynn – who had proposed Meehan as the Parliamentarian candidate. She explained to him that she had taken Dolan's side, not because she admired Sinn Féin, whom she felt were establishing new humbug in place of the old but so as to terminate "the doings of the gang of scoundrels in and out of Parliament who have been dominating Ireland since 1880."[2] That night a crowd assembled in front of Dolan's house and they heard Parnell again describe the Irish Parliamentary party as humbugs and scoundrels.

On the following day, Tuesday she continued in this vein in Kiltyclogher. Referring to local events, in which she participated during the Land War Parnell described the Land League as a gang of scoundrels. She went on to claim that were it not for the Ladies Land League the sham of the Land League would have been recognised long ago and that no Land Purchase Act would have been passed. She accused the I.P.P. of being so servile to the English Liberals that they were dependent on them and were incapable of doing anything for themselves. She felt that only fear of losing Irish support would prompt the Liberals to do anything.

She concluded by asking the electorate to vote not for Dolan or Sinn Féin, but for her sake and the recollection of old times.

Meetings were held on Meehan's behalf in Glenfarne and Kinlough. These were addressed by various MPs such as Sheehy, Hazleton and Kilbride – some of whom were already in the constituency and others who had just left London the previous day. Hazleton in predicting a walkover claimed that in the contest all the nationalists were on one side while there were five or six hundred Unionists on the other. However their presence in North Leitrim gave credibility to the feeling – expressed by the 'Impartial Reporter' and 'Farmer's Journal' – that though unlikely to win Dolan was doing better than expected.

The Parliamentarians also recruited help from Belfast to encourage their own supporters and demoralise those working on Dolan's behalf. These Northerners made their presence felt in Kinlough on Wednesday the 19th of February. Dolan had advertised a meeting to be held in the village but that morning representatives of the U.I.L. travelled from Manorhamilton to Kinlough. On their arrival at about three o'clock Dolan and his companions stopped at Gilmartin's Hotel. What followed is described in 'The Impartial Reporter' and 'Farmers Journal'.

"The local fife and drum band, operating obviously in the interest of Mr. Meehan, paraded the street playing national airs. A brake which had conveyed some friends of Mr Meehan was moved down from a hotel further up the street, and placed nearly opposite Mr Dolan's waggonette. It was a significant move, indicating hostility, and exciting a feeling of uneasiness in the minds of the authorities charged with the preservation of the peace.

As serious disturbances were apprehended additional men were requisitioned from Ballyshannon and Bundoran stations, and twelve or fourteen arrived shortly afterwards, increasing the available force to about twenty. These displayed considerable tact in keeping the opposing crowds from coming into collision. But for their activity conflicts would have frequently occurred.

Meanwhile the Kinlough band was joined by a band from Tullaghan. When Mr.Dermot O'Brien, the League organiser, began to speak from the brake he was interrupted by some of Mr. Dolan's supporters shouting, "Sandy Row". Turning in the direction of his interrupters he warned them that if they did not leave the meeting and cease interrupting he would guarantee they would not leave it alive.

When Mr Dolan appeared in his wagonette shortly afterwards, and was preparing to deliver an address, Mr O'Brien's hearers deserted him, and ran across the street towards the wagonette yelling and groaning apparently for the purpose of preventing Mr Dolan getting a hearing. With a view also to effecting this object several drums were beaten furiously. The noise became deafening and eggs were thrown at Mr. Dolan and his party in the wagonette. These frequently hit their their mark, causing much merriment among Mr Dolan's opponents. Mr Dolan undismayed, struggled to make himself heard, but his efforts were in vain. The task was hopeless. He could not compete with the shrill fifes and the noise of the drums, and although he made a patient and courageous stand against the organised opposition, he was obliged to give up the contest for the moment, but not to entirely abandon it. He renewed the attempt with great pluck a little later, but failed to make his voice heard. Then he shook his fist toward the Meehanites, shouting "Rowdies from Belfast", and asked, "Has it come to this that men should be imported and allowed to conduct themselves in this fashion?" He said his opponents were cowards, who were afraid to give him a fair hearing.

The opposing factions were then drawn close to each other, and a conflict seemed imminent, but the tact of the police again proved effective, and a collision was avoided. The Belfast party began to sing a song ending with the refrain, "The Banner of the United Irish League". They were aided with spirit by the other body of Meehanites, who at a subsequent stage sang "A Nation Once Again". All this time Mr. Dolan held his position, standing in the wagonette, amid a shower of eggs, and an old boot which missed him, and struck one of his friends. Mr Dolan made some observation referring *to "the scum of Belfast". He was answered by a shower of eggs, some of which struck his friends in the wagonette. Mr Dolan apparently much excited, left the wagonette and pushed his way through his own supporters to the cordon of police, and aimed a blow at a man who appeared to be the leader of the Belfast party, but failed to reach him. For a few moments it seemed that his opponents would get beyond control. Sticks were brandished, offensive epithets were freely used, and fears were entertained that the small band of police would be over-powered. Amid the cheers of Mr Meehan's supporters, one of the most prominent among them endeavoured to get at the wagonette, to which Mr. Dolan had in the meantime returned, but he was prevented by the police, who held their ground and successfully resisted the efforts of the two parties to get within striking distance of each other".* [3]

It was also claimed that nearly every man was armed with an ashplant or blackthorn, some had hurley sticks while a bar of iron was carried by one man. Although in the two to three hours that the incident lasted neither faction managed to launch an all out attack and it is evident that neither group was successful in addressing the assembly.

That night some Sinn Féiners accompanied Anna Parnell to Drumshanbo where she intended staying until after the election. However when they arrived a parliamentarian meeting was in progress and Meehan's supporters surrounded the car. Blows were struck but eventually Parnell made her way to the hotel. Subsequently as they left the town her companions were stoned, while when passing through Drumkeerin "they were again the object of a hostile demonstration."

The highlight of Meehan's campaign was a meeting held in Manorhamilton on the same night. There were bands from Killargue, Killasnett and Glencar and the enthusiastic crowd listened to speeches delivered from an upper window in the house of James Lynott, who chaired the meeting. Opening the meeting Lynott commented that thousands had come to endorse the policy of the I.P.P. and he was confident that the Nationalists of North Leitrim would record their support for Meehan.

David Sheehy M.P. said that there was much interest in the political baby Sinn Féin. He described it as unfortunate as its father was "Jack, the Disgrunt", and its mother was "Molly, the Disturber". In his opinion it was a miracle that the baby had been born. He described Sinn Féin as a ragged regiment, a Falstaffian brigade that never did anything and never could do anything. Referring to Lynott as one of the first batch of political prisoners from Manorhamilton he wondered if among Dolan's supporters there was one man who had ever suffered or fought in any way for Ireland. He spoke of Sinn Féin's wish to do away with English law and their desire to have policemen around them occasionally. Sinn Féin had insulted the people of North Leitrim and having made one fool there they expected they could make many. He predicted that Sinn Féin voters would be Unionists and men who had been boycotted. Sheehy illustrated that what he wanted was an emphatic victory which would ensure that Sinn Féin as a political force would be permanently slaughtered in Manorhamilton.

Meehan described the size of the gathering as a fitting answer to Dolan's claim that he, Meehan, dare not hold a meeting in Manorhamilton. He regretted that the people had to take part in a sham battle and claimed that while Dolan was in parliament the people had been forced to fall back on P.A. McHugh. He felt Dolan was more to be pitied than blamed. He was reluctant to criticise his fellow-townsman but he had not been first to introduce personalities. He accused Dolan of ridiculing the Parliamentary Party, the U.I.L. and the A.O.H. while also claiming that he would start a boot factory which had not yet been seen. Meehan blamed the trouble on the existence of £640 which had been subscribed to create faction and it was thought – given his position – that Dolan could be its standard bearer in North Leitrim.

When Meehan had concluded a car carrying some Sinn Féiners arrived at Dolan's door. Although there was some hooting, appeals to the crowd not to have their attention diverted were successful.

F. Cruise O'Brien, President of the Dublin based Young Ireland Branch of the U.I.L. spoke to the gathering in Irish and English. He claimed that abstention from parliament and the establishment of a National Council had been considered unworkable by O'Connell and Smith O'Brien. Cruise O'Brien thought it absurd that Parnell, who had invented Parliamentarianism, had been claimed by Sinn Féin since he had been described as too intense a Parliamentarian. He described a claim that the young men were behind Sinn Féin as untruthful since they "were not going to desert the doctrines of political sanity for those of rhapsodical rhetoric".

A colleague of Cruise O'Brien's in the Young Ireland Branch, W.G. Fallon, also addressed the assembly in both English and Irish – to prove that even a mere United Irish Leaguer could be interested in the revival of the Irish language. He went on that Sinn Féin had only an economic programme and while he was willing to ask for Irish products he also criticised the manufacturers for not advertising their wares better than they did. Fallon felt this form of protection was quite sufficient. He claimed Sinn Féin had not participated in the land struggle but were attacking the organisation and men who had been successful in smashing landlordism. He was certain that the electors would not support a party with no political programme.

Denis Kilbride M.P. stated that all the newspapers in London which hated Ireland such as the 'Times' and 'Standard' were anxious about the election. This was also true of the Orangemen and Unionists but Dillon, Redmond and McHugh were not anxious as they knew what the Nationalists of North Leitrim were made of. Kilbride did not doubt the honesty of the Sinn Féiners but claimed that there were many honest men in the lunatic asylums. There was some anxiety that people might support Dolan out of personal regard for him and his family connections but this would be doing more against the cause of Ireland than all the Orangemen in Belfast were able to do. Kilbride concluded by appealing to the people to encourage Nationalists throughout Ireland, Australia and America by giving Meehan a substantial majority.

Richard Hazleton described the gathering as a suitable conclusion to the great series of meetings which had been held supporting Meehan and the Irish cause. He was delighted that neither Dolan nor his supporters had appeared as they would have been swept off the streets. Although the parliamentarians had not sought a contest, and indeed resented it, he predicted such an emphatic victory that factionism would never again show its face in Leitrim.

In conclusion Lynott said they were at the death of Sinn Féin and would read the burial service over it on Friday. Three cheers were then given for Meehan and the representatives from Dublin. Subsequently the bands with torch lights paraded the town with occasional bursts of booing at Dolan's premises.

Later that night a motor car, in which Dolan had intended touring the constituency on the following day, was damaged after the shed in which the car was housed was entered. The tyres were practically ruined and the hood was tampered with – the damage being estimated at £80. A Meehan supporter who was resident in the Sinn Féin stronghold of Castle Street had several windows in his house broken.

On Thursday evening Dolan and some of his colleagues addressed a gathering in Manorhamilton – the Main Street of which was decorated by a streamer proclaiming... "NO MORE LONDON PARLIAMENT". The Sinn Féin candidate condemned the damage done to the car. There was also much criticism of the behaviour of the Belfast men. Throughout the meeting the Northerners interrupted the speakers and eventually the arrival of Sinn Féin reinforcements from Castle Street resulted in a row which prompted the intervention of the strong police force which was on duty.

A month later evidence was given at Manorhamilton Petty Sessions that Thomas Keany, a member of Manorhamilton Sinn Féin Organisation, was about to throw a piece of iron at some of Meehan's supporters. However Keany's defence was that he was drunk, that he had done nothing and that the weapons had been put in his hands while he was drunk. Not as fortunate was John Gallen, Vice-President of the local National Council. He was charged with throwing a bottle at Meehan's supporters and bound to the peace for twelve months, despite evidence that he too had been struck by a bottle.

Commenting on the campaign "Sinn Féin" of February 22nd.

claimed that the speeches delivered in North Leitrim by the Irish henchmen of the B.N.L.C. were paralleled only by speeches "delivered by the same or similar men seventeen years ago against Charles Stewart Parnell even whilst they beat his sister." It went on that while parliamentarianism might not be successful at procuring compulsory sale, Home Rule or the nationalisation of education, but "at smashing in the head of an Irish manufactured drum, or pouring a jug of water over the head of an Irishwoman it is inimitable." It also claimed that the majority of those who would vote for the parliamentarians would not realise they were supporting the B.N.L.C. – "They will see in the singer of English music hall songs, whom the parliamentary party has nominated, not a puppet of an English party but a conscious Irishman."

A letter from James O'Mara to Dolan was also published. O'Mara claimed that Dolan had gone a long road ignoring the odds against him and by telling the people the truth about Westminster he had everything to lose and nothing to gain. The former M.P. for South Kilkenny described Dolan's programme of religious toleration, industrial progress and agricultural improvement as the road to regeneration. He felt the ideal of a self sufficient Ireland was patriotism as well as sound constitutional doctrine and wished Dolan success.

'The Impartial Reporter' and 'Farmers Journal' described the excitement as reminiscent of elections before the Ballot Act. It condemned the treatment of Anna Parnell, particularly in the light of her role in the land struggle. It felt that if she had come to the constituency earlier her name might have done more for Dolan – whom the Unionist paper considered likely to do better than expected but it still predicted victory for Meehan.

United Irish Parliamentary and National Fund.

39, O'Connell Street, Upper.

Dublin ___18ᵗʰ Decʳ___ 190 7

Nº 4738

RECEIVED FROM *Drumkeerun (Leitrim) U.I.L.*

per *Thomas Nulty, Esq.,* ___ FOR ABOVE FUND

the sum of *Six* ___ POUNDS ___ SHILLINGS

AND ___ PENCE, STERLING.

£ 6 — 0 — 0 per ___

✠ Patrick O'Donnell,
  Bishop of Raphoe,
John E. Redmond,
Stephen O'Mara.

} TRUSTEES.

[signature]

Including £1 from Very Revᵈ P. McMorrow P.P.V.F.
and
£2.7.0 from the Drumkeerun A.O.H.

Chapter 7

When down to Co. Leitrim, they marched the other day
Who but the sister of Parnell should cross them on
their way,
Those heroes nothing daunted, when she came upon the
scene
Fired rotton eggs and spuds at her for the wearin' of the
green.

Given the background to the election and the campaigns conducted by the candidates it was predictable that a huge effort would be made to ensure a high turnout and also that there might be some unsavoury incidents. In Kiltyclogher the appearance in the village for the first time in seven years of an eighty four year old was only slightly less noteworthy than the presence of a ninety year old who hadn't been seen in the village for seventeen years! Surprisingly election day itself was quiet – the only incident of significance occuring when Dolan struck a Mr Martin from Belfast. Although both candidates had agreed to be represented in the polling booths by two personating agents and a sub agent, when Dolan went to cast his vote he objected to Martin's presence claiming that he had been paid to come from Belfast and Dolan challenged his right to be there. Martin replied that Dolan was a liar at which the Sinn Féin candidate struck him. However before he could retaliate Martin"was hustled to an outer apartment, and the incident accordingly closed without any further manifestation of feeling."[1]

Such was the demand on the telegraphic services –reflecting the interest in the election and its result – that the local post office staff had to be re-inforced by supplementary help from Sligo and later from Dublin. Special apparatus was also set up to cope with the demand. Despite these measures Manorhamilton,where the count was to take place, was isolated on the morning of Saturday 24th of February due to a bad storm the previous night during which the wires were torn down. However repairs were quickly carried out to ensure that the result of the election was dispersed throughout the British Isles.

The count itself was a quiet affair. Very few people attended it in the morning and it was midday before any significant number bothered turning up. By that time the result was known unofficially but it was a quarter past one before the returning officer, Wilton Vaugh, announced it officially. Out of a possible 6,324 the actual turnout was 4,335 with seventy five of those who voted spoiling their votes. The result was:

F. Meehan ((Nat)	3103
C.J. Dolan (Sinn Féin)	1157
Majority	1946

On his election Meehan confined himself to thanking the returning officer for the manner in which he had carried out the arrangements in connection with the election. Dolan, having seconded Meehan's proposal of thanks, went on to deliver his interpretation of the result and his hopes for the future. It was, he said, the first time Sinn Féin had challenged the Parliamentarians and he was encouraged by the 1,157 votes which had been recorded, thereby asserting Ireland's right to abstain from the English Parliament. He referred to the four hundred votes which John Martin, the Home Rule movement's first candidate had received. He predicted that as Home Rule had subsequently become Ireland's policy so it would be with Sinn Féin. He also hoped that despite their differences both sides could co-operate in the future and that there would be no bitterness after the election. It was his desire that what both sides had in common would be highlighted while every opportunity to promote Ireland's interests would be taken. By that means the policy which was best for the country and most in keeping with its honour and traditions would prevail. He thanked those who supported him and complimented them on enduring ridicule and scorn for their convictions. Though he had not received the Unionist vote - despite the predictions of the traditionalists – he saw no reason why he should not get the votes of all honest Irishmen. He felt that those who had voted against him did so with reluctance and had abstained from introducing a personal element. He knew they doubted his policy but he believed they would eventually appreciate the views of Sinn Féin. The defeated candidate predicted that an Irish Parliament based on the principles of Sinn Féin would eventually develop. He concluded that those who had not voted illustrated that there were 2,000 people in North Leitrim who still were not decided what was the best policy for the country. Having listened to the returning officer acknowledge the vote of thanks Dolan was accompanied to his house by his uncle Monsignor Dolan.[1]

He subsequently claimed that he would have been more successful if there had not been so many side issues but was satisfied with the vote he got since it was Sinn Féin's first election. He blamed his defeat on clerical opposition, the unity of the Parliamentary Party, the experience of the League's canvassers and the infancy of Sinn Féin.[2]

Later in a conversation with the Press Meehan attributed his success to the intelligence of the people and their determination to support a united pledgebound Parliamentary Party. He also claimed that Sinn Féin, whom he described as "would be dictators of a new policy", – had been campaigning for months while representatives of the Irish Party had only got involved during the run up to the election. McHugh was more outspoken and stated that the two thousand voters who had abstained really supported the parliamentarian candidate but had treated the election as a joke. He claimed the only nationalists who had voted for Dolan had done so on "personal grounds". The M.P. for North Sligo was also of the opinion that the Sinn Féin candidate had received the votes of the Unionist population. He felt nobody supported Dolan's policy i.e Sinn Féin and he broke the returns down as ...

REDMOND	3103
DOLAN	657
UNIONISM	500
FACTION	0

He wished Dolan well and and regretted that he had been duped by political tricksters.[3]

In the press there was mixed reaction to results of the election. The Impartial Reporter and other papers reported that many of the seventy five spoiled votes had been rendered void as they contained uncomplimentary comments about one or other of the candidates. The Unionist paper believed it significant that two thousand people had not voted for the U.I.L. while one thousand votes had actually been cast against it. The mainstream nationalist press welcomed the result. The 'Sligo Champion' predicted that Dolan's actions would result in bitterness, factionism and hatred for years to come. It accused the Sinn Féin candidate of promoting factionism by subsidising the public houses while "political spouters and tramps" were brought in from Wexford, Kerry, Cork, London, Belfast and New York. The 'Irish Independent' felt Sinn Féin could not take much encouragement from the result and called for unity against the common enemy. 'The Irish News' and 'Irish Leader' also welcomed the result. The 'Freeman's Journal' commented on Dolan's graciousness in defeat. It illustrated defects in the Sinn Féin policy and was also of the opinion that Dolan's vote was too small to be used as a foundation for a national movement.

The turnout in the various areas was estimated as follows:

	ON REGISTER	NO. POLLED
DROMAHAIR	1244	798
DRUMKEERIN	1028	657
DRUMNAFILLILA	354	267
DRUMSHANBO	405	298
KESHCARRIGAN	406	265
KILTYCLOGHER	453	365
KINLOUGH	893	632
MANORHAMILTON	1541	1057[4]

'Sinn Féin' reviewed the campaign and the election and the conclusions it reached contrasted sharply with those of the Parliamentarian press. It claimed that if left to themselves the people would not have interfered verbally or physically with Sinn Féin. Belfast hooligans, normally employed as betting mens touts, were blamed for damaging the car placed at Dolan's disposal and attacking Sinn Féiners in Kinlough. They were armed with knuckle dusters, life preservers, revolvers and spiked clubs and paid out of Parliamentary Funds. They wandered through Manorhamilton and attacked isolated Sinn Féin supporters but sought police protection when faced with trouble themselves. It was estimated that the election cost the Parliamentarians between £1500 and £2000. Half this money had been spent on drink and hiring roughs. At every polling station the pubs were bought up and drink was distributed free – while up to £350 was spent on mobs brought from Sligo, Roscommon and Belfast. 'Sinn Féin' saw the election as the beginning of a political era. It believed that the election spelt a revolution more important than that which followed the Clare election in 1828 and predicted that ten years later $5/6$ of Ireland – Catholic and Protestant– would be banded together in National brotherhood. It was felt that future generations would date Ireland's resurrection from the day that 1200 men from the most remote and poorest county in Ireland, voted for Sinn Féin.[5]

At branch level the result was considered encouraging while Dolan was congratulated on his gallant fight. At a meeting of the Central Branch of the National Council on Monday 24th of February Griffith stated that though the significance of the election was not yet appreciated – two days after the result had been declared – it was the first time since the closure of the Irish Parliament that Irishmen declared that England had no right to rule Ireland. He predicted that the fire lit in Leitrim would run through the country until it burned up the last vestige of the rule of the British parliament.[5]

'The Leitrim Guardian' interpreted the result as a victory for Sinn Féin and felt that time was running out for the Parliamentarians to produce tangible results. It commented that Meehan did not enjoy the confidence of the majority of the voters while it felt that it was difficult for Dolan to succeed against the corrupt machinery of the Parliamentarians.[6]

Meehan's success was welcomed by various U.I.L. branches and A.O.H. divisions nationally and internationally in the following weeks. There were band recitals throughout the constituency celebrating his victory. On Monday March 2nd. he had a celebratory dinner with some friends in the Temperance Hotel, Manorhamilton and on the following day he was accompanied to the local train station where he got the 11.10 train to Dublin on the first part of his journey to Westminster.[7] In October 1908 he was instrumental in persuading some estate owners in North Leitrim to sell their lands to the tenants through the Land Commission and thus he himself became owner of part of the estate his ancestors had lost in 1690. He became a treasurer of the Irish Party and represented North Leitrim until 1918. He did not contest the election of that year due to bad health and in 1920 he was awarded the M.B.E by King George V for his work on behalf of Leitrim's poor. He married Molly Hamilton of Dowra, County Cavan but they had no children. In 1903 he took over the family public house in Manorhamilton. He died on December 22nd. 1946.[8]

Having been subsidised throughout the campaign Dolan's newspaper – 'The Leitrim Guardian' – ceased publication on February 29th 1908, with its thirty first edition[9] A meeting of the North Leitrim Executive of the National Council on Friday March 6th was attended by thirty seven delegates representing eight branches – apologies being sent by two other branches. At the meeting, attended by Griffith and Mac Diarmada, Dolan recorded his appreciation of the help they had received from outside the constituency. He and Griffith referred to the small percentage of the electorate who had actually voted for Meehan and described the result as a victory for Sinn Féin. In his address Griffith illustrated how the policy of self-reliance worked and revealed that the National Council had a policy of reviving cottage industry. Instructresses were to be sent down to teach embroidery, knitting etc. and the National Council would get a market for the finished product. It was decided to send samples of Leitrim stone to Dublin with a view to having quarries re-opened. A discussion also took place as to the most suitable industry for Manorhamilton and the possible establishment of a woollen mill, boot factory and tannery were all discussed. The meeting also requested Dolan to go to America later in the year to represent the commercial and political interests of North Leitrim.[10]

Sinn Féin continued to campaign in North Leitrim. They had some successes – in March, Meehan and McHugh received hostile receptions at eviction settlements they attended while Dolan and MacDiarmada were greeted enthusiastically.[11] In June local elections were held and while some Sinn Féin candidates were unsuccessful James Rourke won a seat on their behalf in Drumkeerin. In Manorhamilton, F.E. Meehan claimed he was defeated by J.P. O'Donnell because Sinn Féin and conservatism were against him.[12] During the by-election the parliamentarians regularly referred to the same coalition. 'The Gaelic American' described O'Donnells election as a victory for Sinn Féin.[13]

On a personal level however Dolan's family business was now struggling. Having received financial aid from O'Mara during the campaign the final edition of the 'Leitrim Guardian' advertised a cheap stocktaking sale – and given the circumstances it is not unreasonable to assume that this was merely a means of improving cashflow. Subsequently Dolan sent out bills amounting to £500 but received only £7 in payment. Despite these difficulties the defeated candidate was enthusiastic about the establishment of a boot factory and was confident that £2000 could be raised for that purpose through a joint stock company.[15] In 1909 Dolan went to St.Louis to study the shoe industry. He returned to Ireland in 1911 with the intention of establishing the boot factory and though there were plans to open it –initially in Manorhamilton, then in Dublin and finally in Drogheda – it never got off the ground. After fifteen months he returned to St. Louis, where he married Katherine Kenney in June 1912 and they had one daughter, Alice. Because of his Sinn Féin activities he had, initially, difficulty with his naturalization, but he secured a post at St. Louis University teaching history and languages. He also studied law and in 1917 he began practice as a lawyer. He was appointed Associate City Counsellor in 1921. Seven years later he resigned and though in private practice he served in city hall occasionally until in 1942 he again became an Associate City Counsellor, a post he held until he retired in 1960 at the age of seventy eight. Three years later he inherited a substantial amount of money from an American cousin by marriage– to whom he had been legal adviser.[16]

Politically Dolan became largely redundant after the election. Although he was a member of the executive of Sinn Féin in 1908 and 1909 most of his life was spent in America.[17] In 1921 he was secretary of the Missouri Branch of the *American Association for the Recognition of the Irish Republic*.[18] In America he aligned himself to the Republican Party– influenced he claimed, by Sinn Féin's advocacy of a protectionist policy.[19]

Independent of Dolan, Sinn Féin in North Leitrim was more active immediately after the election than elsewhere in the country. In 1909 outside of Dublin there were seventy four branches and fifteen of these were in Leitrim. However only seven of these fifteen branches had paid the affiliation fee –suggesting that all the momentum created by Dolan in 1907/8 was not maintained.[20] In 1918 James N. Dolan – C.J.'s brother – was elected to the first Dáil where he became Parliamentary Secretary at the Department of Industry and Commerce.

Charles J. Dolan's second marriage —to Gladys Stark took place in 1950. He died in 1963 in St. Louis.[21]

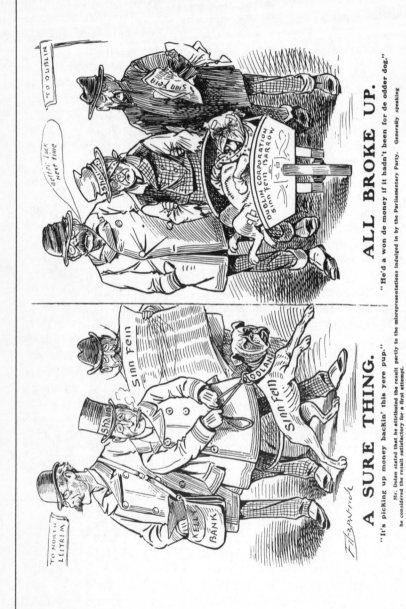

A SURE THING.

"It's picking up money backin' this yere pup."

Mr. Dolan stated that he attributed the result partly to the misrepresentations indulged in by the Parliamentary Party. Generally speaking he considered the result satisfactory for a first attempt.

ALL BROKE UP.

"He'd a won de money if it hadn't been for de odder dog."

Chapter 8

The election is all over
The Sinn Féiners had to go
Another gem to Leitrim's crown
That she won so long ago.

Erin's chivalry cannot be dead, tho' some in Leitrim know
*   it not today*
The venal churls by whom you've been misled for this
*   foul crime a debt will pay*
And Irish manhood rising in its might, will in time to come
*   wipe out the stain*
The mist is drifting and the hills grow bright where burn
*   the watchfires of Sinn Féin.*

When Dolan originally broke ranks with the Parliamentarians they were confident that they would easily win back his seat, when given an opportunity. They didn't feel their position as representatives of the nationalist population was threatened in any way by Sinn Féin. The election would be a means of crushing a "a small inexperienced party of cranks".[1] However the enthusiasm and dedication of Dolan and his supporters were probably more successful in North Leitrim than the traditionalists had anticipated. As a result they themselves were forced to adopt tactics they didn't originally expect to have to employ. Telegrams sent by Joseph Devlin, national secretary of the U.I.L., from Bournemouth towards the end of the campaign demanding that the "constituency be thoroughly worked up" so that the election would "be a triumphant success" illustrate that the Parliamentarians appreciated –as the campaign drew to a close – the importance of the election to them and also Dolan's relatively successful campaign.[2]

Meehan won the election without the support of over half the electorate he represented. It is difficult to say with certainty why the Parliamentarians failed to deliver the blow from which the factionists would never recover – as Meehan had claimed they would.[3] Dolan's name and family reputation were responsible for some of the Sinn Féin votes. His attitude to the Irish Council's Bill and the circumstances of his resignation from the Redmondites were based on principles and may have struck a chord with some of the electorate. His campaign of education had gone on for over six months and the logic of self reliance and withdrawal from Westminster may have influenced some of those who eventually voted for him. He may have received some Unionist votes – the notions of local industry and self reliance appealed to Unionists, many of whom had been alienated early in the campaign by McHugh.* The vitriolic attacks and heavy handed tactics used by some Parliamentarians may have alienated some of their traditional supporters. There was also probably an amount of frustration with the I.P.P. Despite a near monopoly of the domestic political scene and many promises, an Irish parliament was still a dream and all they had achieved was the Irish Councils Bill with little sign of anything better in the forseeable future. Having supported them for nearly forty years some people must have felt the need to transfer their allegiance to some other –any other – nationalist movement.

The 'Kerryman' described the election as a "a Pyrrhic victory for Parliamentarianism" and this is probably fair comment.[4] Having won the election with a substantial majority many parliamentarians may have assumed Sinn Féin would fade into the

---

* The Unionist Impartial Reporter and Farmers Journal (Fermanagh) predicted that Dolan would receive the Unionist vote because of his integrity and parsonality. It also felt that Sinn Féin promotion of local industry and self reliance would appeal to the Unionist population. However the 'Irish Times' felt Sinn Féins attitude to England was "so ridiculous and so disloyal" that loyalists would be unsympathetic to it

background while they would continue to maintain their unassailable role as leaders of the nationalist cause. The margin of their victory was enough to allow the Redmondites continue as the representatives of the vast majority of the Irish people but it was not enough to destroy Sinn Féin and the various shades of opinion it represented – all of which offered alternatives to parliamentarianism. In short the North Leitrim election gave the Redmondites peace of mind but it did not kill off the factionists.

However Asquith's public commitment to Home Rule in December 1909, the abolition of the House of Lords veto and the result of the 1910 general elections, which left the I.P.P. holding the balance of power, all combined to lend Parliamentarianism a momentum it had not enjoyed for many years. While there continued to be differences between them –eleven independent parliamentarians were elected in the January 1910 election – the traditionalists could for the first time be optimistic of achieving their goal– the establishment of a parliament in Dublin.[5] This confidence was justified when in April 1912 Asquith introduced the Third Home Rule Bill to Parliament. Although opposed bitterly by Unionists and altered considerably its implementation seemed assured. As is well documented the Third Home Rule Bill never graduated beyond the British Houses of Parliament. The delay in the Bill's implementation and the development of an alternative nationalist movement resulted in the destruction of the Home Rule movement led by Redmond for almost two decades.

In June 1907 McHugh had written to Redmond that Dolan would be "smitten hip and thigh".[5] On the basis of the election returns and the amount of work done by Dolan and his supporters in a way this was true. The Sinn Féin candidate himself made a huge effort to educate the North Leitrim electorate from June 1907 right up to the time of his defeat. The support he got from the "few cranks and non-entities" from Dublin was impressive and there can be no doubt about the dedication of men such as Walter Cole, Arthur Griffith, Bulmer Hobson and Seán Mac Diarmada in their efforts to secure Dolan's election.[7] As Griffith himself commented "Sinn Féin did not seek the contest in North

Leitrim but it accepts it" and no effort was spared.[8]

Despite the delight with which Griffith greeted the result – he claimed the Leitrim election was the Declaration of Irish Independence– many in Sinn Féin must have been disappointed that they were not more successful. This disappointment was expressed by The O'Rahilly who on hearing the result wrote, "Only today I read in the paper the disheartening result of the Leitrim election. It is disappointing after Sinn Féiners have kept pegging away for nearly a decade, but nations move slowly and it seems hard to enlighten the men of places like Breiffni Ua Ruarc."[10] Probably the main reason for Dolan's relatively small vote –less than one fifth of the electorate cast their votes for him– was his failure to make any impression in large areas of the constituency. This is best illustrated in Dromahair where it was reported that only a local tailor voted for Sinn Féin, and he did so in disgust with a local U.I.L. official who hadn't paid him for a suit he had ordered![11] Dolan's failure to impose himself in these areas may be attributed to the unsympathetic attitude of most of the clergy and a fear that support for Sinn Féin could result in a split among nationalists as bitter as that which followed the fall of Parnell.[12] However the main reasons for his defeat were the U.I.L. and the A.O.H. These were movements with which the people were familiar and their experience in fighting elections ensured that Meehan was practically guaranteed victory. The tactics they used – though possibly alienating some voters – consolidated their hold on others. They appealed to the emotions and comments such as the following left little doubt in the minds of some of the electorate as to Dolan's true motives "there is in my opinion terrible treachery at the bottom of this Sinn Féin policy carefully planned to create disunion amongst the Irish people leading to revolution that would exterminate the Irish people from the country."[13]

The attitude of the mainstream nationalist press was also unhelpful to Dolan and it convinced Griffith of the need to set up a daily paper of his own in an effort to popularise Sinn Féin. In August 1909 the first edition of 'Sinn Féin' as a daily paper appeared. It lasted less than six months and might have been a success were it not for some apparently very basic business errors. When it ceased publication its revenue was 75% of expenditure. Revenue could easily have been increased if Griffith had not insisted on refusing to advertise English manufacturers. Its circulation might also have been increased if other sports besides those governed by the G.A.A. received coverage. That the weekly 'Sinn Féin' continued to be published was also to its disadvantage since many potential readers would have felt that the best articles were likely to be repeated in the weekly edition. Some felt that the large amount of money required for the production of a daily newspaper might be used for more worthwhile purposes. It was also a source of tension between Griffith and the extremists led by Hobson. In an attempt to widen the paper's appeal Griffith adopted a conciliatory attitude to the Unionists and Parliamentarians and this alienated some of his associates in the Sinn Féin movement.[14]

The North Leitrim campaign raised the profile of Sinn Féin to the extent that in August 1908 the Sinn Féin League of America was launched with Robert Temple Emmet –grand-nephew of Robert Emmet – as president and Joseph Mc Garrity as treasurer. Sinn Féiners in Argentina contributed $685 to the daily paper.[15] At home the movement was growing also. There were one hundred and twenty eight branches of Sinn Féin in 1909 compared to twenty one branches in 1906, and even though they may not all have been especially active the increase shows that the message of Sinn Féin was spreading.[16] Indeed shortly after the North Leitrim election a Sinn Féin meeting filled the Dublin Rotunda rooms. Among those present were W.T. Cosgrave, Countess Constance Markievicz, George Russell (A.E.) and Seán O'Casey – perhaps reflecting the type of people who supported Sinn Féin at this stage.[17] That members of the A.O.H. and the U.I.L. disrupted public meetings of Sinn Féin in Dublin in 1909 was an acknowledgement of the potential threat Sinn Féin posed.[18]

Nationalist politics at this time were very fluid – though occasionally differences of opinion could be very emotional. However there was a great deal of movement between the various strands of nationalism from the Parliamentarians right across the spectrum to the I.R.B. In late 1907 William O'Brien contacted Sinn

Féin with a view to participation in a conference of all parties. At first Sinn Féin displayed some interest in the notion but eventually withdrew their support and the proposed conference never got beyond the planning stage. O'Brien again contacted Sinn Féin in March 1909 but Sinn Féin's attitude to Westminster ensured that a united campaign never got off the ground. In December 1909 James Brady, a supporter of O'Brien's, proposed that he and George Gavan Duffy contest Dublin constituencies with the joint backing of the O'Brien/Healyite parliamentary factions and Sinn Féin. Some moderates were sympathetic to this idea as they felt a better Home Rule Bill might be won if Ireland's Nationalists were not exclusively dependent on the Redmondites. However when this proposal was put to the Sinn Féin executive it was rejected.[19] Emphasising the fluidity of Irish politics at this time and the range of opinions held by Sinn Féiners, Eamonn Ceannt claimed in 1910 that "John Redmond and Sinn Féin are the political descendants of Parnell and the Fenians". Though hardly reflecting the feelings of most Sinn Féiners this comment illustrates the range of possibilities available to the nationalist movements in general.[20]

However this period –late 1908-1909 was to be the climax of participation in and influence of Sinn Féin prior to 1918. Its decline may be attributed to the regeneration of the Parliamentarians, the re-organisation of the I.R.B., tensions in Sinn Féin and the emergence of the Irish Volunteers. The bargaining position the I.P.P. found themselves in after the two general elections of 1910 and the removal of the veto of the House of Lords gave the traditionalists a new impetus in the country. Sinn Féin contested neither of these elections mainly due to lack of funds. Griffith claimed they had no desire to increase the bitterness in Ireland while Walter Cole's excuse was that the minority had no right to obstruct the majority. In Connemara Padraic O'Máille attempted to stand for Sinn Féin but was discouraged by Séan Mac Diarmada and others.[21] However Griffith's comment that "Sinn Féin must be ready to form the rallying centre of a disappointed nation" suggests that Sinn Féin were unwilling to allow the Redmondites continue unopposed indefinitely.[22] That he appreciated the difficulties that his own party was experiencing and the potential damage that this attitude could do is reflected in his statement in 1912 following the introduction of the Home Rule Bill, "if a good Bill accepted by Ulster had been introduced I and my party would have disappeared from Ireland. Nobody would have listened to us."[23] The apparent imminence of Home Rule recharged the Parliamentarian batteries and ensured that few of them would follow A.J. Kettle who had resigned from the U.I.L. in 1908 frustrated with the traditionalists' lack of success.[24] Reflecting this national enthusiasm for the Redmondites is Padraic Pearse's attendance at a Parliamentarian demonstration welcoming the Home Rule Bill of 1912, though it was boycotted by Sinn Féin.

The return to Ireland in 1907 of Tom Clarke led to the reorganisation of the I.R.B. This offered a platform to the more militant Sinn Féiners. The I.R.B. claimed a membership of one thousand five hundred in 1909.[25] It is not unreasonable to assume that many in the I.R.B. were at one time sympathetic to Sinn Féin and some people may have been members of both organisations. The militants now had a more suitable platform and this denied Sinn Féin of their services.

Arguably the main cause of Sinn Féin's decline was the tension between the moderates and the extremists or on a more personal level between Griffith and Hobson. Though there were some who respected both points of view and could rally to either cause the differences in opinion were as diverse as those between the moderates in Sinn Féin and the Redmondites. It was inevitable that the rainbow– which was Sinn Féin – could not maintain its momentum, given the range of opinions it represented. While the differences in opinion would have been difficult enough to overcome the distrust that existed between the two factions meant that a parting was inevitable.

In November 1910 the first issue of 'Irish Freedom' was published. This new paper was controlled by the I.R.B., edited by Hobson and managed by MacDiarmada. The establishment of this paper is symbolic of the split between the moderates and extremists. However P.S. O'Hegarty who wrote for 'Irish Freedom' and lectured at Sinn Féin meetings is typical of those who respected both sides.[26]

In September 1910 the 'Peasant" commented that Sinn Féin was "in the last stages of an inglorious existence".[27] At the time, this appeared to be true. It had lost much of the momentum created around the time of the North Leitrim election. Some clubs which once had up to sixty members now had as few as ten members. In January 1908 the movement in London was represented by five branches all of which had ceased to function by 1910. Highlighting the metamorphosis that had occurred in Sinn Féin and also the ultimate humiliation for those extremists still active in the movement, was the fact that part of the 1910 National Convention was allowed into the Mansion House, only on condition that the I.P.P. would not be criticised![28]

While it had never dominated Irish politics, compared to its strength in the wake of the North Leitrim election, Sinn Féin had become marginalised. In 1913 only £40 was raised in subscriptions.[29] However it continued campaigning and educating, though largely removed from mainstream politics. Griffith was active in the organisation of an anti-coronation demonstration in 1911 attended by fifteen thousand people.[30] The annual 'Aonach' or industrial exhibition organised between 1908 and 1916 gained Sinn Féin respect among the Dublin business classes.[31]

In July 1912 five thousand people attended a meeting, organised by Sinn Féín, protesting at the provision in the Home Rule Bill of that year allowing for the British collection of Irish taxes. Consistently, arguments were put forward on ways to improve the Bill. 'Sinn Féin' argued that the success of the Unionist opposition to Home Rule was proof of the effectiveness of the Sinn Féin policy at work. Griffith was also opposed to partition, and made compromise proposals to the Unionists in March 1914 which would have allayed some of their fears about a parliament for all Ireland. The Belfast Trades Council were among those who found some of these proposals interesting. Following the outbreak of War in 1914 and before its suppression 'Sinn Féin' emphasised that Ireland had no quarrel with Germany.[32] The movement was also active in the anti-recruitment drive. While Griffith may have been upset that the momentum created had not been maintained he was now in charge and the party was fulfilling the role he had envisaged for it in 1903 i.e educate the people and work for the establishment of an independent nation. Originally, the notion of contesting elections and competing with the Redmondites had not appealed to him.

However as an organisation with real political clout and of national importance Sinn Féin was in decline. More and more it became a Dublin centred organisation. Griffith himself became its president in 1911 and this reflects the extent to which Sinn Féin was now his organisation. The centralisation of Sinn Féin –which was opposed by the militants – and its withdrawal from parliamentary elections may not have disappointed Griffith but they contributed to the organisation's marginalisation and loss of momentum. In 1910 the organisation established headquarters in a building in Harcourt Street.[33] By October 1915 Sinn Féin's funds were so low that the party could not pay the rent or taxes for the premises.[34]

The emergence of the Irish Volunteers in late 1913 superseded Sinn Féin. Those Parliamentarians who were unhappy with the concessions being offered to the Unionists joined MacNeill's organisation while Hobson and other extremists were instrumental in its establishment. The Volunteers became a vehicle for disgruntled traditionalists while offering a cloak of respectability to the militants, both roles previously fulfilled by Sinn Féin. For the first time in almost half a century the I.R.B. were associated – albeit surreptitiously – with mainstream politicians. Griffith himself was a member of the Volunteers while other Sinn Féiners eg. The O'Rahilly and Ceannt were members of the Volunteer Provisional Committee.[35] Most of the Volunteers were Redmondites and when in late 1914 the Irish Volunteers split, essentially over whether Ireland should participate in the War, the vast majority of them agreed with the Parliamentarian leader and remained loyal to him. They adopted the title 'National Volunteers' while the small minority who sided with McNeill continued as the 'Irish Volunteers'. This latter group became popularly known as Sinn Féin Volunteers. This was probably because for years Sinn Féin was almost the only group who openly offered nationalists an alternative to Parliamentarianism. Initially the split was of significance only in Dublin city.

The National Volunteers were enthusiastic participants in reviews and demonstrations. They saw themselves as defenders of Home Rule or as Joseph Devlin described them the "Irish National Army which had come into being to help the Irish party win Home Rule and help them maintain it once it had been won".Twenty seven thousand of the National Volunteers were among the 132,454 Irishmen who were in the British army in 1915.[36]

In contrast to the Redmondites the Irish Volunteers were largely under the control of the I.R.B., though many of them were unaware of this. Even Eoin Mac Neill, President of the Irish Volunteers, saw his group as gurarantors of Home Rule once the War was over.* Most of the Supreme Council of the I.R.B. saw the War as an opportunity for an insurrection. In contrast Hobson was willing to consider insurrection only if it had a reasonable chance of success. Indeed Griffith and Mac Neill felt the Volunteers should only move against the British if they were pro-voked eg. if an attempt was made to disarm them. The Military Council of the I.R.B. in September 1915 consisted of Tom Clarke, Seán Mac Diarmada, Eamonn Ceannt, Padraic Pearse and Joseph Plunkett and this was the group who were involved in the plan-ning for a rising. Indeed it was only about this time that the full Supreme Council of the I.R.B. become aware of the Military Council's existence. Although in the past some members of the Military Council may have been associated with Sinn Féin by now Ceannt was the only one of them recognised as a leading Sinn Féiner.

Though relatively small in number the Irish Volunteers – or Sinn Féin Volunteers as they were better known– were active. By means of parades, the organisation of O Donovan Rossa's funeral and the campaign against conscription they reached an audience and assumed an importance in excess of what their numbers actu-ally merited‡.

* Mac Neill's own background was Parliamentarian.

Many of the Volunteers weren't advocates of physical force. When the Military Council decided to strike on Easter Sunday 1916 using the Irish Volunteers very few of those who would be involved were informed. Indeed Mc Neill received several assurances that no insurrection was planned. Eventually he was shown a letter – probably prepared by Plunkett and Mac Diarmada – suggesting that the government intended disarming the Volunteers. A government move of this nature was something Mac Neill could not tolerate and he ordered the Volunteers to prepare themselves to resist this development. Hobson was kidnapped –probably by some of his protégées two days before the rising in case he might compromise the rebellion. When Mac Neill discovered that he had been deceived by MacDiarmada in regard to the "government document" concerning the disarming of the Volunteers – and when he learned that a rebellion, which he considered futile, was planned he did all in his power to ensure the Volunteers did not participate. Griffith was one of those used by Mac Neill in his efforts to prevent the rising. And so the Volunteers were ordered by their leader, Mac Neill, not to participate in parades or manoeuveres of any type almost on the very day the I.R.B. had intended using them in a rebellion.

Eventually the insurrection took place on Easter Monday and lasted less than a week. It was described as a Sinn Féin rebellion because the Irish Volunteers who participated in it were popularly known as Sinn Féin Volunteers. Many of those who participated in the rebellion would have been influenced by, and associated with Sinn Féin at some time. The response of the government to the rebellion and the failure to deliver Home Rule alienated the people and gave a momentum to the advanced nationalists which they would hardly have expected a few years previously. It is ironic that when Sinn Féin came to dominate nationalism in 1918 the actual organisation itself had played only a minor role in the main catalyst in its assumption of power – the 1916 rebellion– though its influence on the participants has to be appreciated.With

✢ It is ironic that ODonovan Rossa in his latter years was a supporter of the U.I.L. and actually welcomed Redmond to New York. Yet it was the occasion of his funeral that provided the Irish Volunteers, Redmond's rivals, with their best opportunity to gain the attention of the Irish public.

regard to the rising the term "Sinn Féin" refers to the advanced nationalist movement and not just to Griffith's organisation.

In the aftermath of the North Leitrim election Griffith had complained of violence and intimidation but had predicted that ten years later five-sixths of Ireland would be bonded together in national brotherhood. By 1918 Sinn Féin had become the movement of the people – though hardly by a means envisaged by Griffith – and it was the Parliamentarians who were complaining about violence and intimidation. The North Leitrim election never assumed the importance of the 1828 contest in Clare, despite Griffith's feelings on the matter. However, though the organisation went into decline after a few years, the North Leitrim election did act as a platform for the advanced nationalists and gained them exposure – and thus followers– which they might not otherwise have won. If Dolan had been victorious – always unlikely – the Parliamentarians might have reacted more positively and appreciating the pressure they were under at home might have been more vigilant in ensuring the delivery of Home Rule. On the other hand a successful campaign in North Leitrim might have given Sinn Féin the impetus and momentum it received after the 1916 rising. This new found momentum could have seen Sinn Féin dominate the 1910 elections and possibly an Irish Parliament some years earlier than 1918.

JAMES LYNOTT'S PUBLIC HOUSE, MANORHAMILTON 1904

Appendix 1

National Council (Sinn Féin) Branches December 1907.

John Mitchell Branch, Manorhamilton
C.J. Dolan, M.P, Thomas Rooney, Thomas Gilgunn, P. Fox, John Rooney, F. McSharry, J. Gallen, J. Curneen.

Tarmon:
D. O'Rourke, President; Thomas Judge, Treasurer.

Newbridge:
Michael Mooney, Michael J. Cassidy, Francis Mooney, Francis Flanagan, Michael Dolan.

Cloonclare:
P. Brennan, J. McLoughlin, P. Clarke, M.McMorrow, P. Keany.

Glenfarne: Philip Clancy, B. Maguire, John Cullen, P. Gilgunn.

Kinlough: T. McGowan, M. Tunney, M.O'Dowd, O McGowan, W. Gilmartin.

Ballaghameehan: M. Tucker, Brian McGowan, Henry O'Rourke, James McGurrin, P. Maguire.

Killasnett:
P. Mitchell, Terence Rooney, Hugh McEnroy, James Rooney.

Kiltyclogher:
Patrick McDermott, John McGourty, Michael McMorrow, James Keaney, William Keaney.

Glenade:
F. Rooney, William Rooney, Patrick Rooney, Patrick McGloin, James Clancy.

Glenaniff: Thady Bredin, Patrick Bredin, P. Rooney, J. Connolly.

Appendix 2

Delegates at Convention which selected F.E. Meehan as I.P.P. Candidate: Very Rev. Pat Mc Morrow P.P. Drumkerin, Rev Charles Flynn P.P. Killargue; Rev. Patrick McLoughlin P.P. Glenade; Rev. P. Donoghue C.C. Killargue.

Leitrim Co. Council: P. McManus, Dan Flynn, Patrick Flynn,

Manorhamilton Rural District Council: Thomas McGovern, James O'Rourke, Owen Dolan, James McGoldrick, Charles McMorrow.

Carrick-on-Shannon R.D.C.: John Rynn, John Rutledge, Thomas Flynn, James J. Flynn.

Ballyshannon R.D.C.: James McGurrin, Bernard Connolly, Hugh McGloin, M. Connolly.

U.I.L. Branches

Newbridge: Francis McPartland, Michael Flynn, Pat Watters, Pat McLoughlin, Francis Kerrigan, J. Travers.

Ballinaglera: P. Rynn, P. McGrail, John Flynn, Pat McPartland, T. Loughlin, Anthony Mulvey.

Cloonclare: John Cullen, John McHugh, Frank Keanay, C. Cullen, Frank Keaney, James Regan.

Creevelea: John Gallagher, Farrell McGovern, Thomas Travers, Michael Kilrane, Thomas McSharry, William Gallagher,

Drumkeerin: John O'Rourke, J. O'Donnell, Michael Rogan, Myles McKenna, John Meehan, Tom McNulty,

Drumlease: Patrick Reynolds, H. Kelly, Francis Lynch, James Travers, Patrick O'Connor, Denis Keaney.

Drumshanbo: James McCrann, J. Gildea, James Mahon, John Moran, Francis Mc Nulty, Patrick McLynn.

Glencar: Patrick Lee, J. OConnor, Charles McGauran, T. Ganley, Pat McCann, Francis O'Connor.

Glenfarne: Thomas McGovern, Denis McLoughlin, Pat McGloin, John Keaney, John Gilgunn, M.McHugh.

Killargue: John Travers, Andrew Feeney, Pat Feeney, Thomas Harte, Patrick Lonigan, Lawrence Mc Gowan.

Killasnett: Martin Devaney, Pat McManus, James Rooney, John Feeney, James Connolly, P. Rooney.

Kiltubrid: P. Early, James Connell, Michael Ward, M. Cahill, John Gallagher, Pat Byrne.

Kiltyclogher: Pat McGullion, T. McGurrin, James Dolan, Brian Gallagher, John McMorrow, P. Gallagher.

Kinlough: Terence McGowan, Patrick Devaney, Brian Feely.

Manorhamilton: B.L. Rooney, William McSharry, John Crown, Terence Rooney, Patrick McGuinness, Pat O'Flynn (Solicitor).

Rossinver: William Travers, James O'Rorke, Owen O'Rorke, James Gilmartin, James Gordon, William Meehan.

Tullaghan: E. Doudican, Terence McGowan, John McGowan, Edward Connolly, Pat Rogers, John McGolin.

Killenummery: P. Bartley, J. Sweeny, Pat Keaveny, Thady Kelly, William Conlon, Pat Hannon.

Glenade: Pat McGowan, Owen McGloin, Hugh McGloin, Pat McNulty, Pat Clancy, Roger Rooney.

Ancient Order of Hibernian Divisions

Newtown Manor: Thady Kelly, J. Gilroy, P. Diamond, P. Maguire.

Glencar: Bernard Rooney, Charles Rooney, Pat Gilmartin, Mark Rooney.

Killasnett: L. Rooney, M McDermott, John McViney, James Rooney.

Belhavel: John Flynn, John McMorrow, James Nelson, Thomas Mostyn.

Newbridge: P. Dolan, S. Flynn, T. McManus, F. Flanagan.

Killenummery: W. Lynott, M. Loughlin, J, McGowan, Francis O'Rourke, W. White, John Travers, John Kelly, Denis Meehan.

Drumshanbo: Luke Doyle, Pat McLoughlin, Pat Moran, John P.McKeon.

Creevalea: Stephen Mc Kenna, Pat Flynn, G. Keegan, P. Gallagher.

Ballaghameehan: Bernard Fox, O McGurrin, James McMorrow, William Gilmartin.

Kiltyclogher: Patrick McGovern, Patrick McGloin, Thomas McGovern, John Maguire.

Kinlough: Bernard Connolly, Owen McSharry, Pat Kerrigan, Patrick McGowan.

Drumkeerin: M. Gilmartin, Patrick Flynn, James Fallon.

Glenfarne: J.F. Maguire, John J. Keaney, Michael Maguire, T. Clancy.

Kiltubrid: Pat Byrne, Luke McKiernan, William Conlon, John Mulvey.

Glenade: Felix Cullen, P. Clancy, Edward McGowan, Peter Cullen.

St. Clare's: John Munday, James McEntee, Brian Rooney, Denis McGuinness.

Drumshanbo National Foresters: John Carty, Pat McTernan, John Keane, W. Deignan.

A.O.H. Officers of North Leitrim Executive:

F.E. Meehan, Thomas Fallon Co. C, B. Rooney, J. P McGuinness.

Murrurhamilton, 12 July 1902

My Dear O'Mara,

Notwithstanding newspaper accounts of the treatment I received here in Murrurhamilton, I am still alive and well. I am told that about reports appeared in the London papers of how I was kicked and thumped by an angry crowd. The only person who was so treated was the man who tried to force his way on to the platform. However we have

excitement enough in West Leitrim at present. I intend to resign very soon but I want to have as much time as possible to educate the people. They are coming round and I believe we shall win.

I am bringing out a new local paper on Saturday. I will send you a copy.

Could you come here on Sunday 28th July to address a large meeting here just on the eve of the Poll? You would do us an immense service. The people want to see and

hear you. It would have a
great effect on the
electorate if you were to
come here and publicly
express approval of
my action. Up to the
present the only help I
have here is from boys
and the people want to
see men of standing
connected with us. You
could leave London on
Friday night and get
back on Tuesday morning
if you were in any hurry
to back.

I have some young
fellows here giving
splendid work. I am
busy night and day

and would give anything
for a week's rest. The
strain of this thing is
awful, but no rest for
the wicked and owing
Parliamentarian

I expect Sweetman
to the meeting on 28th July.
Come if possible.
Kind regards to Mrs
O'Mara.

W... & ... .
C. J. Dolan

John Dolan, Merchant
Manorhamilton.

12th July 1907.

My Dear Mr O'Mara,

Notwithstanding newspaper accounts of the treatment I received here in Manorhamilton, I am still alive and well. I am told that absurd reports appeared in the London papers of how I was kicked and thumped by an angry crowd. The only person who was so treated was the man who tried to force his way on to the platform.

However we have excitement enough in North Leitrim at present. I intend to resign very soon but I want to have as much time as possible to educate the people. They are coming round and I believe we shall win. I am bringing out a new local paper on Saturday. I will send you a copy.

Could you come here on Sunday 28th July to address a large meeting here just on the eve of the poll? You would do us an immense service. The people want to see and hear you. It would have a great effect on the electorate if you were to come here and publicly express approval of my action. Up to the present the only help I have is from boys and the people want to see men of standing connected with us. You could leave London on Friday night and get back on Tuesday morning if you were in a hurry back.

I have some young fellows here doing splendid work. I am busy night and day and would give anything for a week's rest. The strain of this thing is awful, but no rest for the wicked and erring Parliamentarian.

I expect Sweetman to the meeting of 28th July. Come if possible. Kind regards to Mrs O'Mara.

Is Mise le meas mór.
C.J. Dolan.

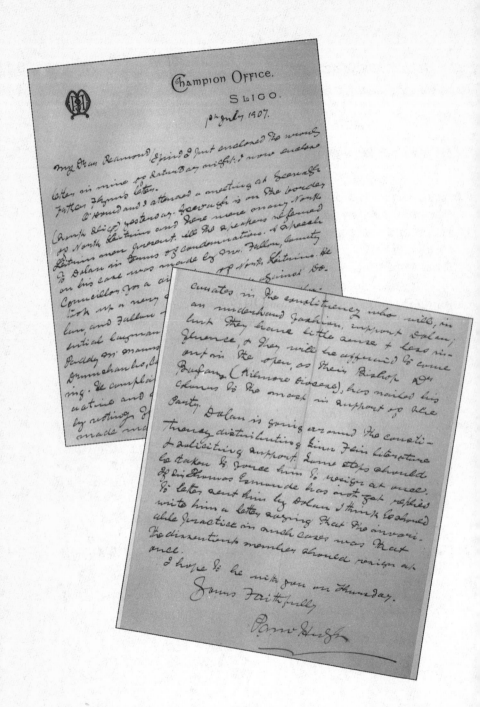

Champion Office.

SLIGO.

1st July 1907.

My Dear Redmond/ I send I just enclosed the words
letter on mine of Saturday night: I now enclose
Father Phynn's letter.

O'Brmd and I attended a meeting at Geenagh
(Co. Sligo) yesterday. Iserrugh is on the border
of North Leitrim and there were many North
Leitrim men present. All the speakers referred
to Dolan in terms of condemnation. A speech
on his case was made by Mr. Fallon, County
Councillor for a ... of North Leitrim. He
... ... against Do-
look up a very ...
lan, and Fallon ...
intial Laymen ...
Paddy Mc Manus ...
Drumshanbo, Co. ...
ing. He complai...
... and ...
by ...
made in...

curates in the constituency who will, in
an underhand fashion, support Dolan;
but they have little sense + less influence, & they will be afraid to come
out in the open, as their Bishop Mcr
Boylan (Kilmore Diocese), has nailed his
colours to the mast in support of the
party. Dolan is going around the constituency distributing Sinn Fein literature
& soliciting support. Some steps should
be taken to force him to resign at once.
If Sir Thomas Esmonde has not got replies
to letters sent him by Dolan I think he should
write him a letter saying that the invariable practice in such cases was that
the dissentient member should resign at
once.

I hope to be with you on Thursday.

Yours Faithfully

Penn Hugh

My Dear Mr. Redmond,

I find I enclosed the wrong letter in mine of Saturday night. I now enclose Fr. Flynn's letter.

O'Dowd and I attended a meeting at Geevagh (South Sligo) yesterday. Geevagh is on the border of North Leitrim and there were many North Leitrim men present. All the speakers referred to Dolan in terms of condemnation. A speech on his case was made by Mr Fallon County Councillor for a division of North Leitrim. He took up a very strong attitude against Dolan and Fallon is, perhaps, the most influential layman politically in North Leitrim. Paddy McManus, Co. Councillor, Drumshanbo, Carrick-on-Shannon was wavering. He complained that the party was inactive and he proposed to improve matters by voting for Dolan. O'Dowd got at him and made matters right. There are two little curates in the constituency who will, in an underhand fashion, support Dolan; but they have little sense and less influence and they will be afraid to come out in the open as their Bishop Dr. Boylan (Kilmore Diocese) has nailed his colours to the mast in support of the party.

Dolan is going around the constituency distributing Sinn Féin literature and soliciting support. Some steps should be taken to force him to resign at once. If Sir Thomas Esmonde has not yet replied to letter sent him by Dolan, I think he should write him a letter saying that the invariable practice in such cases was that the dissenting member should resign at once. I hope to be with you on Thursday.

Your Faithfully
P.A. McHugh.

PAROCHIAL HOUSE
KILLARGY
CO. LEITRIM.

Feast of S.S. Peter & Paul

My Dear P.A.

Tell Mr Redmond that I shall do what I can to have Mr Muldoon selected at Convention. A word from the Leader and another from yourself will go far in this direction. A man whose record and timber so given by Mr Redmond and yourself will do credit to us, the party, and besides lend to the children by every means at our disposal.

Send a message to Mr Jas Keehan to manage to have Peter removed today if really of Party.

I believe after to hear Mr Muldoon they will take to him. He Champion of this date is clear on the Situation of Course there will be no contest for the

good reason that if today Peter side to make up a fight I believe this is a good opportunity afforded by Hibernian meeting to hear Muldoon.

Please assure Mr Redmond of my very best efforts for his now.

Ever thine
C. Lynn

P.a. Mr Hugh Esq M.P.

Feast of S.S. Peter & Paul

My Dear P.A.,

Tell Mr Redmond that I shall do what I can to have Mr. Muldoon selected at 'Convention'. A word from the Leader and another from yourself will go far in this direction. A man, whose record and timber as given by Mr. Redmond and yourself will do credit to us and the party and besides he will not be shaken by every wind of doctrine.

I sent a message to Mr Fras. Meehan to manage to have Resoln. moved today of fidelity to the party.

I believe after they hear Mr Muldoon they will take to him.

The Champion of this date is clear on the situation. Of course there will be no contest for the good reason that it takes two sides to make up a fight. I believe this is a good opportunity afforded by Hibernian meeting to "boom" Muldoon.

Please assure Mr Redmond of my very best efforts for his man and yours.

Ever thine,

C. Flynn.

P.A.Mc Hugh Esq. M.P.

Telegraphic Address:
"Tipperary, Dublin."

UNITED IRISH LEAGUE,

39 Upper O'Connell Street,

Bristol Dublin, 24 Oct 1907

My dear Mr Reilly

I have just learned
with much satisfaction
That Father De Morrow
will preside on Sunday.
Enclosed are resolutions
and the other matter
mentioned

With every good
wish

Yours as ever

D. Sheridan

Thos McReilly

P.S.

I hope our old friends in
Drumkerrin will be
That any attempt
of intended outbreak
at the meeting will
be met with determined
opposition

You will see
Dr Murphy, Dr O'Kenna
and say I will come
I am sure I shall
Dolan or Mr Crowe
put in an appearance
the people might hurt
them out of the town

United Irish League,
39 Upper O'Connell St.,
Dublin

24th Oct 1907

My Dear Mr. Mc Nulty,

I have just learned with much satisfaction that Father McMorrow will preside on Sunday. Enclosed are resolutions and the other matter mentioned.

With every Good Wish,
Yours as ever
D. Johnston

Thos. Mc Nulty Esq.

P.S. I hope our old friends in Drumkeerin will see that any attempt of outsiders to speak at the meeting will be met with determined opposition.

Your will see Mr. Myles McKenna and say how anxious I am that should Dolan or his crowd put in an appearance the people ought to hunt them out of town.

Footnotes

INTRODUCTION

1. F.S.L Lyons 'Ireland Since the Famine', London 1971,p.p 202-203.
2. Robert Kee, 'Volume Two of the Green Flag The Bold Fenian Men, London 1972 p.125
3. Ibid, p.126 quoting Denis Gwynn, Life of John Redmond, London 1932 p.84.
4. Joseph Lee'The Modernisation of Irish Society 1848 - 1918", Dublin 1973 p.123.
5. Lyons F.S.L. op cit p.212
6. Lyons F.S.L. op cit p.217
7. Ibid pp 260 - 263
8. Ibid pp 209- 210 and Mark Tierney 'Modern Ireland', Dublin 1972 p.35.
9. Lyons F.S.L. op. cit p.p. 211 - 214
10. Lyons F.S.L. op.cit p.p.217 - 223
11. LYONS F.S.L. op. cit 225 - 226
12. KEE op.cit. p.133: quoting report on lecture The Revival of Irish Literature, London 1894
13. LYONS F.S.L. p.p. 228 - 229
14. Ibid p.247
15. Ibid p 248
16. RICHARD DAVIS "Arthrur Griffith and Non-Violent Sinn Féin," Dublin 1974 p 5 quoting Sinn Féin, 7th October 1911.
17. F.S.L. LYONS op. cit p.248
18. GEORGE LYONS, 'Some Recollections of Griffith and His Times", Dublin 1923 p.8
19. DAVIS R. op cit p.17 quoting 'United Irishman' 15th March 1900, quoted by P.S. O'Hegarty, 'A History of Ireland Under the Union', London 1952 p. 37 and 'The United Irishman 6th October 1900 and December 1st. 1900.
20. LYONS G. op.cit p.9 and p.p. 34 - 42 and Davis R. op cit p.40.
21. DAVIS R. op cit p.p. 19, 20 quoting United Irisman 8th August 1903 and Lyons F.S.L. Op cit p.255.
22. DAVIS R. op cit p.p. 20-21 quoting Irish World 12th Februarry 1876.
23. LYONS F.S.L. op citp.p. 255- 256 quoting P.S. O'Hegarty: Ireland Under the Union p.p. 643 - 653. (George Lyons in Some Recollections of Griffith and His Times p.63 credits a nun with suggesting the name).
24. DAVIS R. op. cit p.24: quoting P.S. O'Hegarty to Gavan Duffy, 11th April 1907, George Gavan Duggy papers National Library of Ireland.
25. Ibid P.28-32
26 Ibid P.33 quoting Peasant 13th April 1907.

27. Ibid p.33 quoting Peasant 11th May 1907.
28. LYONS F.S.L. op. cit p. 256
29. KEE op cit p.159 quoting F.S.L. Lyons John Dillon, A Biography, London 1968 p.288.
30. LYONS GEORGE op. cit p 66.
31. *Sinn Féin*, January 4th 1908.
32. DAVIS R. op cit p.23
33. LYONS F.S.L. op cit. p.p. 263 - 265.
34. LYONS George op. cit p.p 66-67.

CHAPTER ONE

1. St Louis Post Dispatch August,10 1930 and St. Louis Globe Democrat Magazine, October 30th 1927. David W. Millar, "Church, State and Nation In Modern Ireland 1898-1921" Dublin 1973, page 218, quoting the 'Impartial Reporter and Farmer's Journal' July 4th 1901
2. James O Mara papers M.S.21545 National Library of Ireland; Letters from Dolan to O'Mara on January 18th 1908 and one 14th 1908 thanking O'Mara for cheques received which helped business over critical periods.
3. Sligo Champion January 13, January20, February 10th, March 3rd, 1906.
4. Mrs. P. Wilson Manorhamilton, 1981 said James Dolan swore her husband Pat into the I.R.B.
5. Patricia Lavelle: James O'Mara a staunch Sinn Féiner 1873 - 1948, Dublin 1961
6. F.S.L. Lyons, 'The Irish Parliamentary Party 1890-1910', London 1951,pp 107 - 109.
7. Ibid, p.p.117 - 122
8. Freeman's Journal June 22nd. 1907.

CHAPTER TWO

1. F.S.L. Lyons, "Ireland Since the Famine', London 1971, p 262 quoting J.J. Bergin, History of the Ancient Order of Hibernians, Dublin, 1910.
2. Seán O Luing 'Art Ó Gríofa Beathaisnéís', Dublin 1953, p.171 quoting Nationality 19/5/1917
3. Ibid p.171
4. Sligo Champion February 29th 1908.
5. O Luing, op cit p.165.
6. Sligo Champion July 6 1907.
7. Redmond Papers MS 15203 National Library of Ireland, Mc Hugh to Redmond June 25th and June 29th.
8. Freeman's Journal July 8th 1907.
9. Sinn Féin February 15th 1908
10. James O Mara Papers MS21544 Dolan to O'Mara July 1907.

CHAPTER THREE

1. Patricia Lavelle: James O'Mara A staunch Sinn Féiner 1873 - 1948, Dublin, 1961 p.p. 85-87.
2. ibid p.p.85-87.
3. 'Sligo Champion' July, 27 1907.
4. Sinn Féin July 27, 1907 and 'Frreeman's Journal, July 23 1907.
5. 'Freeman's Journal', July 29 1907.
6. 'Sligo Champion', August 3, 1907.
7. Sinn Féin, August 3rd 1907
8. 'Sligo Champion', August 17 and August 24 1907.
9. Lavelle op. cit p.90 and'Freeman's Journal' July 22nd 1907.
10. 'Freeman's Journal, August 15, August 23, August 24 1907.
11. 'Sligo Champion', August17 and 24 1907.
12. 'Sinn Féin', Auguat 24, 1907.
13. 'Sligo Champion', August 24 1907.
14. 'Sinn Féin', August 24 and August 31 1907.
15. 'Sligo Champion', September 14 1907.
16. 'Sinn Féin', September 7 1907.
17. 'Sligo Champion', September 7 and September 21 1907.
18. 'Sinn Féin', September 7, 1907.

CHAPTER FOUR

1. 'Freeman's Journal', September 20th 1907.
2. 'Sinn Féin' September 28th October 12th, 1907.
3 'Sligo Champion' September 14, September 28 and October 12th 1907.
4. 'Sinn Féin' October 5th 1907.
5. 'Freeman's Journal', September 5th 1907 and 'Impartial Reporter' and 'Farmer's Journal ', September 12 1907.
6. 'Sligo Champion', November 2 and 'Leitrim Observer' Novermber 2 1907 and 'Impartial Reporter' and 'Farmers Journal, October 31st 1907.
7. "Sligo Champion', November 9th 1907.
8. 'Sinn Féin', November 9th and November 16th 1907.
9. Fr. Harper C.C. in letter to 'Sinn Féin', November 16th 1907.

CHAPTER FIVE

1. 'Sinn Féin', November 23rd 1907.
2. 'Sligo Champion', December 14th 1907.
3. 'Sinn Féin', February 1st, 1908.
4. 'Sligo Champion', December 14th 1907.
5. 'Sinn Féin', December 21st 1907, December 28th 1907 and Sligo Champion January 4th 1908. 'Impartial Reporter' and Farmers Journal., January 2nd 1908.
6. 'Sligo Champion', December 21st 1908.
7. 'Sinn Féin' January 25th 1908. 'The Sligo Champion', January 18th claimed that

only three Sinn Féin candidates were successful.

8. Davis R. 'Arthur Griffith and Non Violent Sinn Féin', 1974 p77.
9. 'Impartial Reporter' and 'Farmer's Journal', January 23rd 1908.
10. 'Freemans Journal', January 15th 1908.
11. "Impartial Reporter' and 'Farmer's Journal' January 16th 1908.
12. 'Sligo Champion', Febrauray 1st 1908.
13. 'Freeman's Journal', January 30th , February 6th and February 7th 1908.
14. 'Sligo Champion' February 8th 1908 and February 15th 1908.
15. 'Sligo Champion', February 1st 1908.
16 'Sinn Féin, February 8th and 15th 1908
17. 'Sinn Féin, February 1st, 15th and 22nd 1908.
18. 'Sligo Champion', February 8th and 15th 1908.
19 'Sinn Féin', Februray 8th and 15th 1908.
20. 'Sligo Champion', February 1st and 8th 1908.
21. 'Leitrim Observer' February 15th 1908.
22. 'Leitrim Observer, February 15th 1908 and 'Sligo Champion' February 15th 1908.

CHAPTER SIX

1. 'Impartial Reporter' and 'Farmers Journal', Feb 20th ,1908.
2. Sinn Féin, Feb 22nd., 1908.
3. Letter from Anna Parnell to Mrs Lennon, Kiltyclogher.
4. 'Impartial Reporter' and 'Farmers Journal', February 27th 1908.
5. Irish Daily Telegraph, Friday February 21st. 1908.
6. Ibid.

CHAPTER SEVEN

1. 'Impatial Reporter and Farmers Journal, Feb 27th 1908.' Freemans Journal', Feb. 21st., 22nd, 23rd, 1908. 'Sligo champion', February 29th 1908.
2. 'Impartal Reporter' and 'Farmers Journal', March 5th 1908.
3. 'Sligo Champion', Feb 29th, 1908 and 'Impartial Reporter' and 'Farmer's Journal', Feb 27th 1908.
4. 'Sligo Champion', Feb, 29th 1908.
5. 'Sinn Féin', Feb 29th 1908.
6. 'Sinn Féin', March 7th 1908.
7. 'Impartial Reporter' and 'Freeman's Journal', Feb 27th and 'Sligo Champion', March 7th 1908.
8. Correspondence with Patrick Meehan, Portlaoise.
9. O'Mara Papers M.S. 21545, National Library of Ireland, Dolan to O'Mara June 1908.
10 'Sinn Féin', March 14th 1908.
11. 'Sinn Féin', March 21st. 1908.
12. 'Leitrim Observer June 6th 1908.

13. 'Gaelic American' June 2oth 1908.
14. O' Mara Papers MS 21545.
15. Davis R. op. cit. p. 51.
16. 'St. Louis Post Dispatch', August 10th 1930; June 2 1960; June 1 1960; March 23rd and 24th 1963.
17. Davis, R. op cit P.174.
18. Lavelle, op cit page 77;
19. 'St. LouisPost Dispatch' p.p. 83,84.
21. Susanne Stark-Kline, St. Louis, stepdaughter of Charles J. Dolan (1992)

CHAPTER EIGHT
1. J. Keaveney to U.I.L. meeting at Cloonclare, quoted in 'Sligo Champion', September 14th 1907.
2. Telegrams quoted in 'Sinn Féin', March 7th, 1908.
3. Meehan to campaign meeting in Manorhamilton quoted in 'Sligo Champion, Feb 15th 1908.
4. Quoted in Davis R. op. cit. P. 49.
5. Lyons F.S.L. 'Ireland Since The Famine', p. 263.
6. Redmond Papers, MS 15203 National Library of Ireland.
7. 'Sligo Champion', February 15th 1908.
8. 'Sinn Féin' June 29th 1907.
9. 'Sinn Féin' February 29th 1908.
10. O'Mara Papers MS 21545, National Library of Ireland; O Rahilly to O'Mara 1908.
11. O' Luing, Seán, Art Ó Gríofa Beatháisnéis 1953.
12. See 'Sligo Champion' June 29th 1907 report of Killargue U.I.L.
13. Letter from P.J. McAndrew, London qoted in 'Sligo Champion', August 24th 1907.
14. O Luing, op. cit p.p. 182-18 and Davis R op cit p.p. 59-62.
15. Davis R. op. cit p. 50 quoting 'Gaelic American' 4th July and 15th August 1908.
16. ibid. p81/82 quoting 'Sinn Féin' 8th September 1906 and Annual Register 28th August 1909.
17. ibid. p. 50 quoting 'Gaelic American' 11th April 1908.
18. ibid. p. 78.
19. ibid. p.p. 59-63.
20. ibid p.64 quoting 'Irish Nation and Peasant 3rd February 1910.
21. ibid. p.p. 51-52.
22. Robert Kee 'The Bold Fenian Men' p. 160 quoting 'Sinn Féin', 8th October 1910; 14th October 1911; 18th February 1911.
23. Davis R. op. cit. p.51 quoting A. Denson. Letters from A.E. p. 114 (AE to Arthur Balfour 1st June 1916.)

Arthur Balfour 1st June 1916.)

24. ibid. p. 50 and 54 quoting 'Gaelic American' 9th May 1908 and 'Sinn Féin' 6th April 1912.
25. ibid p. 82.
26 ibid p.p. 67,68.
27 ibid p. 65 quoting 'Irish Nation and Peasant 15th February 1910.
28. ibid p.66 and p.p. 82-85.
29. ibid p. 86
30. ibid 68 quoting 'Sinn Féin' 13th May 1911.
31. ibid. p. 69.
32. ibid p.p. 55,56,57, quoting 'Sinn Féin' 27th July 1912 and 7th March 1914, 28th March 19184, 8th August 1914.
33. ibid. p.85
34. Kee R. op. cit. quoting 'Freeman's Journal' 11th May 1915.
35. Davis R. op. cit. quoting Gaelic American', 13th December 1913.
36. Kee. R. op cit. p.p. 223-231 quoting 'Freeman's Journal' 19th October 1914.

Bibliography

NEWSPAPERS
'The Leitrim Observer'
'The Sligo Champion'
The 'Impartial Reporter' and 'Farmers Journal' (Fermanagh)
'The Freeman's Journal'
'Sinn Féin'
'Irish Daily Telegraph'
'The Gaelic American'
'St. Louis Post-Dispatch'
'St. Louis Globe-Democrat Magazine'

PERIODICALS/MAGAZINES
'Leprechaun'
'Breifne' Vol II No. 9

MANUSCRIPTS
Redmond Papers MS 15203 National Library of Ireland.
James O'Mara papers MS 21544/5 National Library of Ireland.
Drumkeerin U.I.L. Minute Book by kind permission of John McNulty.
Letter of Anna Parnell by kind permission of Mrs Mary Slevin.

ORAL SOURCES
Mrs Pat Wilson. R.I.P., Manorhamilton.
Patrick F. Meehan, Portlaoise.

BOOKS
Joseph Lee 'The Modernisation of Irish Society' – 1848 - 1918, Dublin 1973.
Padraic Colum, 'Arthur Griffith, Dublin 1974.
Bulmer Hobson, 'Ireland Yesterday and Tomorrow' Tralee 1968.
Robert Kee, 'The Bold Fenian Men', London 1972
George Lyons, 'The Irish Parliamentary Party 1890 - 1910., London 1951
David Millar, 'Church, State and Nation in Modern Ireland', Dublin 1973.
Sean O Luing, 'Art O'Griofa', Dublin 1953.
Patricia Lavelle, 'James O'Mara, a Staunch Sinn Féiner, 1873 - 1948', Dublin 1961.
Proinnsios O'Conluain, 'Sean T, Dublin 1963.
Robert Mitchell Henry, 'The Evolution of Sinn Fein', Dublin . Not dated.
Mark Tierney, 'Modern Ireland', Dublin 1972.
F.S.L. Lyons,'John Dillon, 'London, 1968. 'Ireland Since the Famine' (1971). 'The
      Irish parliamentary Party' 1890-1910, 1951
W. O'Brien, 'An Olive Branch In Ireland', 1910.
George Lyons 'Some Recollections of Griffith and his Times' 1923.

Index

DRUMLIN PUBLICATIONS
NURE, MANORHAMILTON, CO. LEITRIM, IRELAND

NORTH LEITRIM IN FAMINE TIMES No 1 £3 Irl/G.B $ 10 U.S.

Proinnsíos Ó Duigneáin. The horror of the Great Famine in this area of the West of Ireland is vividly recalled – A time when three plots beside the workhouse had to be provided for the scores who died during the worst years.

NORTH LEITRIM: THE LAND WAR AND
THE FALL OF PARNELL No 3 £3.50 Irl/G.B $10 U.S.

Proinnsíos Ó Duigneáin. A comprehensive account of the struggle for the land up to 1891. It also contains a fascinating picture of the area after the Parnell divorce case. p.b. 80 pages.

DROMAHAIRE: STORY AND PICTURES £5 $15 U.S.

Proinnsíos Ó Duigneáin. A social history of the village of Dromahaire and the surrounding area 1800 - 1890 p.b. 125 pages

O RUAIRC OF BREIFNE £16 Irl/G.B $45 U.S.
Lady Betty mc Dermot: *A beautifully bound, comprehensive account of the O Rourke family from earliest times. h.b. 220 pages.*

THE FIRST SINN FÉIN ELECTION 1908 NO 4 £ 4.95Irl/GB $15 U.S.
Ciarán Ó Duibhir: *This is a detailed account of the first election ever contested by the party founded by Arthur Griffith – the party which ten years later swept the boards and gave expression to the ideals of the men and women of 1916.*

MEMORIES

Lily O'Hagan *evokes in her poetry the beauty of the* £5 Irl/G.B $15 U.S.
Leitrim countryside and recalls the sad and the joyful occasions of her life.

NORTH LEITRIM IN LAND LEAGUE TIMES No 2 £3 Irl/G.B $10 U.S.

Proinnsíos Ó Duigneáin. North Leitrim 1880 - 1884. A comprehensive account of th organisation in the area including the Ladies Land League.

ALL PRICES INCLUDE AIRMAIL POST AND PACKING